**Ben Stacy Jerrik (Ed.)**

# Denotational Semantics of the Actor Model

**Ben Stacy Jerrik (Ed.)**

# Denotational Semantics of the Actor Model

## Denotational semantics, Domain theory, Actor model

**Part Press**

**Imprint**

Permission is granted to copy, distribute and/or modify this document under the terms of the GNU Free Documentation License, Version 1.2 or any later version published by the Free Software Foundation; with no Invariant Sections, with the Front-Cover Texts, and with the Back- Cover Texts. A copy of the license is included in the section entitled "GNU Free Documentation License".

All parts of this book are extracted from Wikipedia, the free encyclopedia (www.wikipedia.org).

You can get detailed informations about the authors of this collection of articles at the end of this book. The editors (Ed.) of this book are no authors. They have not modified or extended the original texts.

Pictures published in this book can be under different licences than the GNU Free Documentation License. You can get detailed informations about the authors and licences of pictures at the end of this book.

The content of this book was generated collaboratively by volunteers. Please be advised that nothing found here has necessarily been reviewed by people with the expertise required to provide you with complete, accurate or reliable information. Some information in this book maybe misleading or wrong. The Publisher does not guarantee the validity of the information found here. If you need specific advice (f.e. in fields of medical, legal, financial, or risk management questions) please contact a professional who is licensed or knowledgeable in that area.

Any brand names and product names mentioned in this book are subject to trademark, brand or patent protection and are trademarks or registered trademarks of their respective holders. The use of brand names, product names, common names, trade names, product descriptions etc. even without a particular marking in this works is in no way to be construed to mean that such names may be regarded as unrestricted in respect of trademark and brand protection legislation and could thus be used by anyone.

Cover image: www.ingimage.com
Concerning the licence of the cover image please contact ingimage.

Publisher:
Part Press is a trademark of
International Book Market Service Ltd., 17 Rue Meldrum, Beau Bassin, 1713-01 Mauritius
Email: info@bookmarketservice.com
Website: www.bookmarketservice.com

Published in 2012

Printed in: U.S.A., U.K., Germany. This book was not produced in Mauritius.

**ISBN: 978-613-5-65778-4**

# Contents


## Articles

| | |
|---|---|
| Denotational_semantics_of_the_Actor_model | 1 |
| Denotational_semantics | 8 |
| Domain_theory | 15 |
| Actor_model | 20 |
| Partially_ordered_set | 33 |
| Indeterminacy_in_concurrent_computation | 38 |
| Lambda_calculus | 41 |

## References

| | |
|---|---|
| Article Sources and Contributors | 57 |
| Image Sources, Licenses and Contributors | 58 |

# Denotational_semantics_of_the_Actor_model

The **denotational semantics of the Actor model** is the subject of denotational domain theory for Actors. The historical development of this subject is recounted in [Hewitt 2008b].

## Actor fixed point semantics

The denotational theory of computational system semantics is concerned with finding mathematical objects that represent what systems do. Collections of such objects are called domains. The Actor uses the domain of event diagram scenarios. It is usual to assume some properties of the domain, such as the existence of limits of chains (see cpo) and a bottom element. Various additional properties are often reasonable and helpful: the article on domain theory has more details.

A domain is typically a partial order, which can be understood as an order of definedness. For instance, given event diagram scenarios $x$ and $y$, one might let "$x \leq y$" mean that "$y$ extends the computations $x$".

The mathematical denotation denoted by a system $S$ is found by constructing increasingly better approximations from an initial empty denotation called $\perp_S$ using some denotation approximating function $\mathbf{progression}_S$ to construct a denotation (meaning ) for $S$ as follows:

$$\mathbf{Denote}_S \equiv \sqcup_{i \in \omega} \mathbf{progression}_S^{i}(\perp_S).$$

It would be expected that $\mathbf{progression}_S$ would be *monotone*, *i.e.*, if $x \leq y$ then $\mathbf{progression}_S(x) \leq \mathbf{progression}_S(y)$. More generally, we would expect that

$$\text{If } \forall i \in \omega \ \ x_i \leq x_{i+1}, \text{ then } \mathbf{progression}_S(\sqcup_{i \in \omega} x_i) = \sqcup_{i \in \omega} \mathbf{progression}_S(x_i)$$

This last stated property of $\mathbf{progression}_S$ is called $\omega$-continuity.

A central question of denotational semantics is to characterize when it is possible to create denotations (meanings) according to the equation for $\mathbf{Denote}_S$. A fundamental theorem of computational domain theory is that if $\mathbf{progression}_S$ is $\omega$-continuous then $\mathbf{Denote}_S$ will exist.

It follows from the $\omega$-continuity of $\mathbf{progression}_S$ that

$$\mathbf{progression}_S(\mathbf{Denote}_S) = \mathbf{Denote}_S$$

The above equation motivates the terminology that $\mathbf{Denote}_S$ is a *fixed point* of $\mathbf{progression}_S$.

Furthermore this fixed point is least among all fixed points of $\mathbf{progression}_S$.

## Compositionality in programming languages

An important aspect of denotational semantics of programming languages is compositionality, by which the denotation of a program is constructed from denotations of its parts. For example consider the expression "<expression$_1$> + <expression$_2$>". Compositionality in this case is to provide a meaning for "<expression$_1$> + <expression$_2$>" in terms of the meanings of <expression$_1$> and <expression$_2$>.

The Actor model provides a modern and very general way the compositionality of programs can be analyzed. Scott and Strachey [1971] proposed that the semantics of programming languages be reduced to the semantics of the lambda calculus and thus inherit the denotational semantics of the lambda calculus. However, it turned out that concurrent computation could not be implemented in the lambda calculus (see Indeterminacy in concurrent computation). Thus there arose the problem of how to provide modular denotational semantics for concurrent programming languages. One solution to this problem is to use the Actor model of computation. In Actor model, programs are Actors that are sent `Eval` messages with the address of an environment (explained below) so that programs inherit their denotational semantics from the denotational semantics of the Actor model (an idea published in Hewitt [2006]).

## Environments

Environments hold the bindings of identifiers. When an environment is sent a `Lookup` message with the address of an identifier **x**, it returns the latest (lexical) binding of **x**.

As an example of how this works consider the lambda expression <L> below which implements a tree data structure when supplied with parameters for a `leftSubTree` and `rightSubTree`. When such a tree is given a parameter message `"getLeft"`, it return `leftSubTree` and likewise when given the message `"getRight"` it returns `rightSubTree`.

```
λ(leftSubTree, rightSubTree)
  λ(message)
     if (message == "getLeft") then leftSubTree
     else if (message == "getRight") then rightSubTree
```

Consider what happens when an expression of the form `"(<L> 1 2)"` is sent an `Eval` message with environment **E**. One semantics for application expressions such as this one is the following: <L>, 1 and 2 are each sent `Eval` messages with environment **E**. The integers 1 and 2 immediately reply to the `Eval` message with themselves.

However, <L> responds to the `Eval` message by creating a closure Actor (process) **C** that has an address (called *body*) for <L> and an address (called *environment*) for **E**. The Actor `" (<L> 1 2) "` then sends **C** the message **[1 2]**.

When **C** receives the message **[1 2]**, it creates a new environment Actor **F** which behaves as follows:

1. When it receives a `Lookup` message for the identifier `leftSubTree`, it responds with 1
2. When it receives a `Lookup` message for the identifier `rightSubTree`, it responds with 2
3. When it receives a `Lookup` message for any other identifier, it forwards the `Lookup` message to **E**

The Actor (process) **C** then sends an `Eval` message with environment **F** to the following actor (process):

```
λ(message)
  if (message == "getLeft") then leftSubTree
  else if (message == "getRight") then rightSubTree
```

## Arithmetic expressions

For another example consider the Actor for the expression `"<expression`$_1$`> + <expression`$_2$`>"` which has addresses for two other actors (processes) `<expression`$_1$`>` and `<expression`$_2$`>`. When the composite expression Actor (process) receives an `Eval` message with addresses for an environment Actor **E** and a customer **C**, it sends `Eval` messages to `<expression`$_1$`>` and `<expression`$_2$`>` with environment **E** and sends **C** a new Actor (process) **C$_0$**. When **C$_0$** has received back two values **N$_1$** and **N$_2$**, it sends **C** the value **N$_1$ + N$_2$**. In this way, the denotational semantics for process calculi and the Actor model provide a denotational semantics for `"<expression`$_1$`> + <expression`$_2$`>"` in terms of the semantics for `<expression`$_1$`>` and `<expression`$_2$`>`.

## Other programming language constructs

The denotational compositional semantics presented above is very general and can be used for functional, imperative, concurrent, logic, *etc.* programs (see [Hewitt 2008a]). For example it easily provides denotation semantics for constructs that are difficult to formaize using other approaches such as delays and futures.

# Clinger's Model

In his doctoral dissertation, Will Clinger developed the first denotation semantics for the Actor model.

## The domain of Actor computations

Clinger [1981] explained the domain of Actor computations as follows:

> The augmented Actor event diagrams [see Actor model theory] form a partially ordered set < **Diagrams**, ≤ > from which to construct the power domain $P$[**Diagrams**]  (see the section on Denotations below). The augmented diagrams are partial computation histories representing "snapshots" [relative to some frame of reference] of a computation on its way to being completed. For $x,y \in$**Diagrams**, $x \leq y$  means $x$  is a stage the computation could go through on its way to $y$. The completed elements of **Diagrams**  represent computations that have terminated and nonterminating computations that have become infinite. The completed elements may be characterized abstractly as the maximal elements of **Diagrams**  [see William Wadge 1979]. Concretely, the completed elements are those having non pending events. Intuitively, **Diagrams**  is not ω-complete because there exist increasing sequences of finite partial computations
>
> in which some pending event remains pending forever while the number of realized events grows without bound, contrary to the requirement of finite [arrival] delay. Such a sequence cannot have a limit, because any limit would represent a completed nonterminating computation in which an event is still pending.
>
> To repeat, the actor event diagram domain **Diagrams**  is incomplete because of the requirement of finite arrival delay, which allows any finite delay between an event and an event it activates but rules out infinite delay.

## Denotations

In his doctoral dissertation, Will Clinger explained how power domains are obtained from incomplete domains as follows:

From the article on Power domains: $P$[D]  is the collection of downward-closed subsets of domain D  that are also closed under existing least upper bounds of directed sets in D. Note that while the ordering on $P$[D]  is given by the subset relation, least upper bounds do not in general coincide with unions.

> For the actor event diagram domain **Diagrams**, an element of $P$[**Diagrams**]  represents a list of possible initial histories of a computation. Since for elements $x$  and $y$  of **Diagrams**, $x \leq y$  means that $x$  is an initial segment of the initial history $y$, the requirement that elements of $P$[**Diagrams**]  be downward-closed has a clear basis in intuition.
>
> ...
>
> Usually the partial order from which the power domain is constructed is required to be ω-complete. There are two reasons for this. The first reason is that most power domains are simply generalizations of domains that have been used as semantic domains for conventional sequential programs, and such domains are all complete because of the need to compute fixed points in the sequential case. The second reason is that ω-completeness permits the solution of recursive domain equations involving the power domain such as
>
> which defines a domain of resumptions [Gordon Plotkin 1976]. However, power domains can be defined for any domain whatsoever. Furthermore the power domain of a domain is essentially the power domain of its

ω-completion, so recursive equations involving the power domain of an incomplete domain can still be solved, provide the domains to which the usual constructors (+, ×, →, and *) are applied are ω-complete. It happens that defining Actor semantics as in Clinger [1981] does not require solving any recursive equations involving the power domain.

In short, there is no technical impediment to building power domains from incomplete domains. But why should one want to do so?

In *behavioral semantics*, developed by Irene Greif, the meaning of program is a specification of the computations that may be performed by the program. The computations are represented formally by Actor event diagrams. Greif specified the event diagrams by means of causal axioms governing the behaviors of individual Actors [Greif 1975].

Henry Baker has presented a nondeterministic interpreter generating instantaneous schedules which then map onto event diagrams. He suggested that a corresponding deterministic interpreter operating on sets of instantaneous schedules could be defined using power domain semantics [Baker 1978].

The semantics presented in [Clinger 1981] is a version of behavioral semantics. A program denotes a set of Actor event diagrams. The set is defined extensionally using power domain semantics rather than intensionally using causal axioms. The behaviors of individual Actors is defined functionally. It is shown, however, that the resulting set of Actor event diagrams consists of exactly those diagrams that satisfy causal axioms expressing the functional behaviors of Actors. Thus Greif's behavioral semantics is compatible with a denotational power domain semantics.

Baker's instantaneous schedules introduced the notion of *pending events*, which represent messages on the way to their targets. Each pending event must become an actual (realized) arrival event sooner or later, a requirement referred to as *finite delay*. Augmenting Actor event diagrams with sets of pending events helps to express the finite delay property, which is characteristic of true concurrency [Schwartz 1979].

## Sequential computations form an ω-complete subdomain of the domain of Actor computations

In his 1981 dissertation, Clinger showed how sequential computations form a subdomain of concurrent computations:

> Instead of beginning with a semantics for sequential programs and then trying to extend it for concurrency, Actor semantics views concurrency as primary and obtains the semantics of sequential programs as a special case.
>
> ...
>
> The fact that there exist increasing sequences without least upper bounds may seem strange to those accustomed to thinking about the semantics of sequential programs. It may help to point out that the increasing sequences produced by sequential programs all have least upper bounds. Indeed, the partial computations that can be produced by sequential computation form an ω-complete subdomain of the domain of Actor computations **Diagrams**. An informal proof follows.
>
> > From the Actor point of view, sequential computations are a special case of concurrent computations, distinguishable by their event diagrams. The event diagram of a sequential computation has an initial event, and no event activates more than one event. In other words, the activation ordering of a sequential computation is linear; the event diagram is essentially a conventional execution sequence. This means that the finite elements of **Diagrams**
> >
> > corresponding to the finite initial segments of a sequential execution sequence all have exactly one pending event, excepting the largest, completed element if the computation terminates. One property of the augmented event diagrams domain < **Diagrams**, ≤ > is that if x≤y and x≠y, then some pending

event of x is realized in y. Since in this case each $x_i$ has at most one pending event, every pending event in the sequence becomes realized. Hence the sequence

has a least upper bound in **Diagrams** in accord with intuition.

The above proof applies to all sequential programs, even those with choice points such as guarded commands. Thus Actor semantics includes sequential programs as a special case, and agrees with conventional semantics of such programs.

## The Timed Diagrams Model

Hewitt [2006b] published a new denotational semantics for Actors based on Timed Diagrams. The Timed Diagrams model stands in contrast to Clinger [1981] which constructed an ω-complete power domain from an underlying incomplete diagrammatic domain, which did not include time. The advantage of the domain Timed Diagrams model is that it is physically motivated and the resulting computations have the desired property of ω-completeness (therefore unbounded nondeterminism) which provides guarantee of service.

### Domain of Timed Actor Computations

Timed Diagrams denotational semantics constructs an ω-complete computational domain for Actor computations. In the domain, for each event in an Actor computation, there is a delivery time which represents the time at which the message is delivered such that each delivery time satisfies the following conditions:

1. The delivery time is a positive rational number that is not the same as the delivery time of any other message.
2. The delivery time is more than a fixed δ greater than the time of its activating event. It will later turn out that the value of δ doesn't matter. In fact the value of δ can even be allowed to decrease linearly with time to accommodate Moore's Law.

The Actor event timed diagrams form a partially ordered set **<TimedDiagrams, ≤>**. The diagrams are partial computation histories representing "snapshots" (relative to some frame of reference) of a computation on its way to being completed. For d1,d2ε**TimedDiagrams**, d1≤d2 means d1 is a stage the computation could go through on its way to d2 The completed elements of **TimedDiagrams** represent computations that have terminated and nonterminating computations that have become infinite. The completed elements may be characterized abstractly as the maximal elements of **TimedDiagrams**. Concretely, the completed elements are those having no pending events.

*Theorem:* **TimedDiagrams** is an ω-complete domain of Actor computations i.e.,

1. If D⊆**TimedDiagrams** is directed, the least upper bound ⊔D exists; furthermore ⊔D obeys all the laws of Actor model theory.
2. The finite elements of **TimedDiagrams** are countable where an element xε**TimedDiagrams** is finite (isolated) if and only if D⊆**TimedDiagrams** is directed and x≤VD, there exists dεD with x≤d. In other words, x is finite if one must go through x in order to get up to or above x via the limit process.
3. Every element of **TimedDiagrams** is the least upper bound of a countable increasing sequence of finite elements.

## Power domains

Definition: The domain $\langle$Power["'TimedDiagrams]"', $\subseteq\rangle$ is the set of possible initial histories M of a computation such that

1. M is downward-closed, *i.e.,* if d$\varepsilon$M, then $\forall$d'$\varepsilon$TimedDiagrams d'$\leq$d $\Rightarrow$ d'$\varepsilon$M
2. M is closed under least upper bounds of directed sets, i.e. if D$\subseteq$M is directed, then VD$\varepsilon$M

Note: Although Power[**TimedDiagrams**] is ordered by $\subseteq$, limits are not given by U. I.e.,

$$(\forall i \in \omega \ M_i \leq M_{i+1}) \ _{i \in \omega} M_i \ \subseteq \sqcup_{i \in \omega} M_i$$

E.g., If $\forall$i $d_i\varepsilon$**TimedDiagrams** and $d_i \leq d_{i+1}$ and $M_i = \{d_k \mid k \leq i\}$ then

$$\sqcup_{i \in \omega} M_i = \ _{i \in \omega} M_i \ \{ \ \sqcup_{i \in \omega} d_i \ \}$$

*Theorem:* Power [**TimedDiagrams**] is an $\omega$-complete domain.

## Concurrency Representation Theorem

An Actor computation can progress in many ways. Let d be a diagram with next scheduled event e and X $\equiv$ $\{e'|e{-}\approx{\rightarrow}_{1\text{-message}} e'\}$ (see Actor model theory), Flow(d) is defined to be the set of all timed diagrams with d and extensions of d by X such that

1. the arrival all of the events of X has been scheduled where
2. the events of X are scheduled in all possible orderings among the scheduled future events of d
3. subject to the constraint that each event in X is scheduled at least $\delta$ after e and every event in X is scheduled at least once in every $\delta$ interval after that.

(Recall that $\delta$ is the minimum amount of time to deliver a message.)

Flow(d) $\equiv$ {d} if d is complete.

Let S be an Actor system, Progression$_S$ is a mapping

    Power[**TimedDiagrams**]$\rightarrow$Power[**TimedDiagrams**]

    $\text{Progression}_S(M) \equiv U_{d\varepsilon M} \text{Flow}(d)$

*Theorem:* Progression$_S$ is $\omega$-continuous.

*I.e.,* if $\forall$i $M_i \subseteq M_{i+1}$ then $\text{Progression}_S(\sqcup_{i\varepsilon\omega} M_i) = \sqcup_{i\varepsilon\omega} \text{Progression}_S(M_i)$

Furthermore the least fixed point of Progression$_S$ is given by the Concurrency Representation Theorem as follows:

$$\sqcup_{i\varepsilon\omega} \text{Progression}_S^{\ i}(\perp_S)$$

where $\perp_S$ is the initial configuration of S.

The denotation Denote$_S$ of an Actor system S is the set of all computations of S.

Define the *time abstraction* of a timed diagram to be the diagram with the time annotations removed.

*Representation Theorem:* The denotation Denote$_S$ of an Actor system S is the time abstraction of

$$\sqcup_{i\varepsilon\omega} \text{Progression}_S^{\ i}(\perp_S)$$

Using the domain **TimedDiagrams**, which is $\omega$-complete, is important because it provides for the direct expression of the above representation theorem for the denotations of Actor systems by directly constructing a minimal fixed point.

The criterion of continuity for the graphs of functions that Scott used to initially develop the denotational semantics of functions can be derived as a consequence of the Actor laws for computation as shown in the next section.

# References

- Dana Scott and Christopher Strachey. Toward a mathematical semantics for computer languages Oxford Programming Research Group Technical Monograph. PRG-6. 1971.
- Irene Greif. *Semantics of Communicating Parallel Professes* MIT EECS Doctoral Dissertation. August 1975.
- Joseph E. Stoy, *Denotational Semantics: The Scott-Strachey Approach to Programming Language Semantics.* MIT Press, Cambridge, Massachusetts, 1977. (A classic if dated textbook.)
- Gordon Plotkin. *A powerdomain construction* SIAM Journal of Computing September 1976.
- Edsger Dijkstra. *A Discipline of Programming* Prentice Hall. 1976.
- Krzysztof R. Apt, J. W. de Bakker. *Exercises in Denotational Semantics* MFCS 1976: 1-11
- J. W. de Bakker. *Least Fixed Points Revisited* Theor. Comput. Sci. 2(2): 155-181 (1976)
- Carl Hewitt and Henry Baker *Actors and Continuous Functionals* Proceeding of IFIP Working Conference on Formal Description of Programming Concepts. August 1–5, 1977.
- Henry Baker. *Actor Systems for Real-Time Computation* MIT EECS Doctoral Dissertation. January 1978.
- Michael Smyth. *Power domains* Journal of Computer and System Sciences. 1978.
- C.A.R. Hoare. *Communicating Sequential Processes* CACM. August, 1978.
- George Milne and Robin Milner. *Concurrent processes and their syntax* JACM. April, 1979.
- Nissim Francez, C.A.R. Hoare, Daniel Lehmann, and Willem-Paul de Roever. *Semantics of nondeterminism, concurrency, and communication* Journal of Computer and System Sciences. December 1979.
- Nancy Lynch and Michael J. Fischer. *On describing the behavior of distributed systems* in Semantics of Concurrent Computation. Springer-Verlag. 1979.
- Jerald Schwartz *Denotational semantics of parallelism* in Semantics of Concurrent Computation. Springer-Verlag. 1979.
- William Wadge. *An extensional treatment of dataflow deadlock* Semantics of Concurrent Computation. Springer-Verlag. 1979.
- Ralph-Johan Back. *Semantics of Unbounded Nondeterminism* ICALP 1980.
- David Park. *On the semantics of fair parallelism* Proceedings of the Winter School on Formal Software Specification. Springer-Verlag. 1980.
- Will Clinger, *Foundations of Actor Semantics*. MIT Mathematics Doctoral Dissertation, June 1981. (Quoted by permission of author.)
- Carl Hewitt What is Commitment? Physical, Organizational, and Social [1] Pablo Noriega .et. al. editors. LNAI 4386. Springer-Verlag. 2007.

# References

[1] http://www.pcs.usp.br/~coin-aamas06/10_commitment-43_16pages.pdf

# Denotational_semantics

In computer science, **denotational semantics** (initially known as **mathematical semantics** or **Scott–Strachey semantics**) is an approach to formalizing the meanings of programming languages by constructing mathematical objects (called *denotations*) which describe the meanings of expressions from the languages. Other approaches to providing a formal semantics of programming languages include axiomatic semantics and operational semantics.

Broadly speaking, denotational semantics is concerned with finding mathematical objects called domains that represent what programs do. For example, programs (or program phrases) might be represented by partial functions, or by Actor event diagram scenarios, or by games between the environment and the system: these are all general examples of domains.

An important tenet of denotational semantics is that *semantics should be compositional*: the denotation of a program phrase should be built out of the denotations of its subphrases.

## Historical development

Denotational semantics originated in the work of Christopher Strachey and Dana Scott in the late 1960s.[1] As originally developed by Strachey and Scott, denotational semantics provided the denotation (meaning) of a computer program as a function that mapped input into output.[2] To give denotations to recursively defined programs, Scott proposed working with continuous functions between domains, specifically complete partial orders. As described below, work has continued in investigating appropriate denotational semantics for aspects of programming languages such as sequentiality, concurrency, non-determinism and local state.

Denotational semantics have been developed for modern programming languages that use capabilities like concurrency and exceptions, e.g., Concurrent ML,[3] CSP,[4] and Haskell.[5] The semantics of these languages is compositional in that the denotation of a phrase depends on the denotations of its subphrases. For example, the meaning of the applicative expression f(E1,E2) is defined in terms of semantics of its subphrases f, E1 and E2. In a modern programming language, E1 and E2 can be evaluated concurrently and the execution of one of them might affect the other by interacting through shared objects causing their denotations to be defined in terms of each other. Also, E1 or E2 might throw an exception which could terminate the execution of the other one. The sections below describe special cases of the semantics of these modern programming languages.

### Denotations of recursive programs

A denotational semantics is given to a program phrase as a function from an environment (that has the values of its free variables) to its denotation. For example, the phrase n*m produces a denotation when provided with an environment that has binding for its two free variables: n and m. If in the environment n has the value 3 and m has the value 5, then the denotation is 15.

A function can be modeled as denoting a set of ordered pairs where each ordered pair in the set consists of two parts (1) an argument for the function and (2) the value of the function for that argument. For example the set of order pairs {[0 1] [4 3]} is the denotation of a function with value 1 for argument 0, value 3 for the argument 4, and is otherwise undefined.

The problem to be solved is to provide denotations for recursive programs that are defined in terms of themselves such as the definition of the factorial function as

```
factorial ≡ λ(n) if (n==0) then 1 else n*factorial(n-1).
```

A solution is to build up the denotation by approximation starting with the empty set of order pairs (which in set theory would be written as { }). If { } is plugged into the above definition of factorial then the denotation is {[0 1]}, which is a better approximation of factorial. Iterating: If {[0 1]} is plugged into the definition then the denotation is

{[0 1] [1 1]}. So it is convenient to think of an approximation to `factorial` as an input F in the following way:

```
λ(F) λ(n) if (n==0) then 1 else n*F(n-1).
```

It is instructive to think of a chain of "iterates" where $F^i$ indicates $i$-many applications of $F$.

- $F^0(\{\})$ is the totally undefined partial function {}
- $F^1(\{\})$ is the function {[0 1]} that is defined at 0, to be 1, and undefined elsewhere;
- $F^5(\{\})$ is the function {[0 1] [1 1] [2 2] [3 6] [4 24]}

The least upper bound of this chain is the full `factorial` function which can be expressed as follows where the symbol "⊔" means "least upper bound":

## Denotational semantics of non-deterministic programs

The concept of power domains has been developed to give a denotational semantics to non-deterministic sequential programs. Writing $P$ for a power domain constructor, the domain $P(D)$ is the domain of non-deterministic computations of type denoted by $D$.

There are difficulties with fairness and unboundedness in domain-theoretic models of non-determinism.[6] See Power domains for nondeterminism.

## Denotational semantics of concurrency

Many researchers have argued that the domain theoretic models given above do not suffice for the more general case of concurrent computation. For this reason various new models have been introduced. In the early 1980s, people began using the style of denotational semantics to give semantics for concurrent languages. Examples include Will Clinger's work with the actor model; Glynn Winskel's work with event structures and petri nets;[7] and the work by Francez, Hoare, Lehmann, and de Roever (1979) on trace semantics for CSP.[8] All these lines of inquiry remain under investigation (see e.g. the various denotational models for CSP[4] ).

Recently, Winskel and others have proposed the category of profunctors as a domain theory for concurrency.[9] [10]

## Denotational semantics of state

State (such as a heap) and simple imperative features can be straightforwardly modeled in the denotational semantics described above. All the textbooks below have the details. The key idea is to consider a command as a partial function on some domain of states. The denotation of "`x:=3`" is then the function that takes a state to the state with 3 assigned to x. The sequencing operator "`;`" is denoted by composition of functions. Fixed-point constructions are then used to give a semantics to looping constructs, such as "`while`".

Things become more difficult in modelling programs with local variables. One approach is to no longer work with domains, but instead to interpret types as functors from some category of worlds to a category of domains. Programs are then denoted by natural continuous functions between these functors.[11] [12]

## Denotations of data types

Many programming languages allow users to define recursive data types. For example, the type of lists of numbers can be specified by

```
datatype list = Cons of (Nat, list) | Empty.
```

This section deals only with functional data structures that cannot change. Conventional imperative programming languages would typically allow the elements of such a recursive list to be changed.

For another example: the type of denotations of the untyped lambda calculus is

```
datatype D = (D → D)
```

The problem of *solving domain equations* is concerned with finding domains that model these kinds of datatypes. One approach, roughly speaking, is to consider the collection of all domains as a domain itself, and then solve the recursive definition there. The textbooks below give more details.

Polymorphic data types are data types that are defined with a parameter. For example, the type of $\alpha$ lists is defined by

```
datatype a list = Cons of (a, a list) | Empty.
```

Lists of numbers, then, are of type Nat list, while lists of strings are of type String list.

Some researchers have developed domain theoretic models of polymorphism. Other researchers have also modeled parametric polymorphism within constructive set theories. Details are found in the textbooks listed below.

A recent research area has involved denotational semantics for object and class based programming languages.[13]

## Denotational semantics for programs of restricted complexity

Following the development of programming languages based on linear logic, denotational semantics have been given to languages for linear usage (see e.g. proof nets, coherence spaces) and also polynomial time complexity.[14]

## Denotational semantics of sequentiality

The problem of full abstraction for the sequential programming language PCF was, for a long time, a big open question in denotational semantics. The difficulty with PCF is that it is a very sequential language. For example, there is no way to define the parallel-or function in PCF. It is for this reason that the approach using domains, as introduced above, yields a denotational semantics that is not fully abstract.

This open question was mostly resolved in the 1990s with the development of game semantics and also with techniques involving logical relations.[15] For more details, see the page on PCF.

## Denotational semantics as source-to-source translation

It is often useful to translate one programming language into another. For example, a concurrent programming language might be translated into a process calculus; a high-level programming language might be translated into byte-code. (Indeed, conventional denotational semantics can be seen as the interpretation of programming languages into the internal language of the category of domains.)

In this context, notions from denotational semantics, such as full abstraction, help to satisfy security concerns.[16] [17]

# Abstraction

It is often considered important to connect denotational semantics with operational semantics. This is especially important when the denotational semantics is rather mathematical and abstract, and the operational semantics is more concrete or closer to the computational intuitions. The following properties of a denotational semantics are often of interest.

1. **Syntax independence**: The denotations of programs should not involve the syntax of the source language.
2. **Soundness**: All observably distinct programs have distinct denotations;
3. **Full abstraction**: Two programs have the same denotations precisely when they are observationally equivalent. For semantics in the traditional style, full abstraction may be understood roughly as the requirement that "operational equivalence coincides with denotational equality". For denotational semantics in more intensional models, such as the Actor model and process calculi, there are different notions of equivalence within each model, and so the concept of full abstraction is a matter of debate, and harder to pin down. Also the mathematical structure of operational semantics and denotational semantics can become very close.

Additional desirable properties we may wish to hold between operational and denotational semantics are:

1. **Constructivism**: Constructivism is concerned with whether domain elements can be shown to exist by constructive methods.
2. **Independence of denotational and operational semantics**: The denotational semantics should be formalized using mathematical structures that are independent of the operational semantics of a programming language; However, the underlying concepts can be closely related. See the section on Compositionality below.
3. **Full completeness** or **definability**: Every morphism of the semantic model should be the denotation of a program.[18]

## Compositionality

An important aspect of denotational semantics of programming languages is compositionality, by which the denotation of a program is constructed from denotations of its parts. For example consider the expression "7 + 4". Compositionality in this case is to provide a meaning for "7 + 4" in terms of the meanings of "7", "4" and "+".

A basic denotational semantics in domain theory is compositional because it is given as follows. We start by considering program fragments, i.e. programs with free variables. A *typing context* assigns a type to each free variable. For instance, in the expression $(x + y)$ might be considered in a typing context $(x{:}\mathtt{nat}, y{:}\mathtt{nat})$. We now give a denotational semantics to program fragments, using the following scheme.

1. We begin by describing the meaning of the types of our language: the meaning of each type must be a domain. We write $\tau$ for the domain denoting the type $\tau$. For instance, the meaning of type $\mathtt{nat}$ should be the domain of natural numbers: $\mathtt{nat} = {}_\perp$.
2. From the meaning of types we derive a meaning for typing contexts. We set $x_1{:}\tau_1,\ldots, x_n{:}\tau_n = \tau_1 \times \ldots \times \tau_n$. For instance, $x{:}\mathtt{nat}, y{:}\mathtt{nat} = {}_\perp \times {}_\perp$. As a special case, the meaning of the empty typing context, with no variables, is the domain with one element, denoted 1.
3. Finally, we must give a meaning to each program-fragment-in-typing-context. Suppose that $P$ is a program fragment of type $\sigma$, in typing context $\Gamma$, often written $\Gamma \vdash P{:}\sigma$. Then the meaning of this program-in-typing-context must be a continuous function $\Gamma \vdash P : \sigma : \Gamma \to \sigma$. For instance, $\vdash 7{:}\mathtt{nat}{:} 1 \to {}_\perp$ is the constantly "7" function, while $x{:}\mathtt{nat}, y{:}\mathtt{nat} \vdash x{+}y{:}\mathtt{nat}: {}_\perp \times {}_\perp \to {}_\perp$ is the function that adds two numbers.

Now, the meaning of the compound expression (7+4) is determined by composing the three functions $\vdash 7{:}\mathtt{nat}{:} 1 \to {}_\perp$, $\vdash 4{:}\mathtt{nat}{:} 1 \to {}_\perp$, and $x{:}\mathtt{nat}, y{:}\mathtt{nat} \vdash x{+}y{:}\mathtt{nat}: {}_\perp \times {}_\perp \to {}_\perp$.

In fact, this is a general scheme for compositional denotational semantics. There is nothing specific about domains and continuous functions here. One can work with a different category instead. For example, in game semantics, the category of games has games as objects and strategies as morphisms: we can interpret types as games, and programs as strategies. For a simple language without general recursion, we can make do with the category of sets and functions. For a language with side-effects, we can work in the Kleisli category for a monad. For a language with state, we can work in a functor category. Milner has advocated modelling location and interaction by working in a category with interfaces as objects and *bigraphs* as morphisms.[19]

## Semantics versus implementation

According to Dana Scott [1980]:

> *It is not necessary for the semantics to determine an implementation, but it should provide criteria for showing that an implementation is correct.*

According to Clinger (1981):

> *Usually, however, the formal semantics of a conventional sequential programming language may itself be interpreted to provide an (inefficient) implementation of the language. A formal semantics need not always provide such an implementation, though, and to believe that semantics must provide an implementation leads to confusion about the formal semantics of concurrent languages. Such confusion is painfully evident when the presence of unbounded nondeterminism in a programming language's semantics is said to imply that the programming language cannot be implemented.*

## Connections to other areas of computer science

Some work in denotational semantics has interpreted types as domains in the sense of domain theory which can be seen as a branch of model theory, leading to connections with type theory and category theory. Within computer science, there are connections with abstract interpretation, program verification, and model checking.

Monads were introduced to denotational semantics as a way of organising semantics, and these ideas have had a big impact in functional programming (see monads in functional programming).

## References


[1] Dana S. Scott. Outline of a mathematical theory of computation. Technical Monograph PRG-2, Oxford University Computing Laboratory, Oxford, England, November 1970.

[2] Dana Scott and Christopher Strachey. *Toward a mathematical semantics for computer languages* Oxford Programming Research Group Technical Monograph. PRG-6. 1971.

[3] John Reppy "Concurrent ML: Design, Application and Semantics" in Springer-Verlag, Lecture Notes in Computer Science, Vol. 693. 1993

[4] A. W. Roscoe. "The Theory and Practice of Concurrency" Prentice-Hall. Revised 2005.

[5] Simon Peyton Jones, Alastair Reid, Fergus Henderson, Tony Hoare, and Simon Marlow. "A semantics for imprecise exceptions" Conference on Programming Language Design and Implementation. 1999.

[6] Paul Blain Levy: Amb Breaks Well-Pointedness, Ground Amb Doesn't. Electr. Notes Theor. Comput. Sci. 173: 221-239 (2007)

[7] Event Structure Semantics for CCS and Related Languages. DAIMI Research Report, University of Aarhus, 67 pp., April 1983.

[8] Nissim Francez, C.A.R. Hoare, Daniel Lehmann, and Willem-Paul de Roever. *Semantics of nondeterminism, concurrency, and communication* Journal of Computer and System Sciences. December 1979.

[9] Gian Luca Cattani, Glynn Winskel. Profunctors, open maps and bisimulation. *Mathematical Structures in Computer Science*, 15(3):553–614 (2005).

[10] Mikkel Nygaard, Glynn Winskel: Domain theory for concurrency. *Theoretical Computer Science*, 316(1):153–190 (2004).

[11] Peter W. O'Hearn, John Power, Robert D. Tennent, Makoto Takeyama. Syntactic control of interference revisited. *Electr. Notes Theor. Comput. Sci.* 1. 1995.

[12] Frank J. Oles. *A Category-Theoretic Approach to the Semantics of Programming*. PhD thesis, Syracuse University, New York, USA. 1982.

[13] Bernhard Reus, Thomas Streicher. Semantics and logic of object calculi. *Theor. Comput. Sci.*, 316(1):191–213 (2004).

[14] P. Baillot. Stratified coherence spaces: a denotational semantics for Light Linear Logic (ps.gz) Theoretical Computer Science , 318 (1-2), pp. 29-55, 2004.

[15] P. W. O'Hearn and J. G. Riecke. Kripke Logical Relations and PCF, *Information and Computation*, 120(1):107–116 (July 1995).

[16] Martin Abadi. Protection in programming-language translations. Proc. of ICALP'98. LNCS 1443. 1998.

[17] Andrew Kennedy. Securing the .NET programming model. Theoretical Computer Science, 364(3). 2006

[18] Curien, Pierre-Louis (2007). "Definability and Full Abstraction". *Electronic Notes in Theoretical Computer Science* (Papers in honour of Gordon Plotkin: Elsevier) 172: 301–310. doi:10.1016/j.entcs.2007.02.011.

[19] The Space and Motion of Communicating Agents. Robin Milner. Cambridge University Press, 2009, ISBN 978-0-521-73833-0, 2009 draft (https://blog.itu.dk/SMDS-F2010/files/2010/04/milner-2009-the-space-and-motion-of-communicating-agents.pdf).

## Further reading

Textbooks

- Joseph E. Stoy, *Denotational Semantics: The Scott-Strachey Approach to Programming Language Semantics*. MIT Press, Cambridge, Massachusetts, 1977. (A classic if dated textbook.)
- Carl Gunter, "Semantics of Programming Languages: Structures and Techniques". MIT Press, Cambridge, Massachusetts, 1992. (ISBN 978-0262071437)
- Glynn Winskel, *Formal Semantics of Programming Languages*. MIT Press, Cambridge, Massachusetts, 1993. (ISBN 978-0262731034)
- R. D. Tennent, *Denotational semantics*. Handbook of logic in computer science, vol. 3 pp 169–322. Oxford University Press, 1994. (ISBN 0-19-853762-X)
- S. Abramsky and A. Jung: *Domain theory* (http://www.cs.bham.ac.uk/~axj/pub/papers/handy1.pdf). In S. Abramsky, D. M. Gabbay, T. S. E. Maibaum, editors, Handbook of Logic in Computer Science, vol. III. Oxford University Press, 1994. (ISBN 0-19-853762-X)
- David A. Schmidt, *Denotational semantics: a methodology for language development*, Allyn and Bacon, 1986, ISBN 0-205-10450-9 (out or print now; free electronic version available (http://www.cis.ksu.edu/~schmidt/text/densem.html))

Lecture notes

- Glynn Winskel. *Denotational Semantics* (http://www.cl.cam.ac.uk/~gw104/dens.pdf). University of Cambridge.

Other references

- Irene Greif. *Semantics of Communicating Parallel Processes* MIT EECS Doctoral Dissertation. August 1975.
- Gordon Plotkin. *A powerdomain construction* SIAM Journal on Computing September 1976.
- Edsger Dijkstra. *A Discipline of Programming* Prentice Hall. 1976.
- Krzysztof R. Apt, J. W. de Bakker. *Exercises in Denotational Semantics* MFCS 1976: 1-11
- J. W. de Bakker. *Least Fixed Points Revisited* Theoretical Computer Science 2(2): 155-181 (1976)
- Carl Hewitt and Henry Baker *Actors and Continuous Functionals* (http://www.lcs.mit.edu/publications/pubs/pdf/MIT-LCS-TR-194.pdf) Proceeding of IFIP Working Conference on Formal Description of Programming Concepts. August 1–5, 1977.
- Henry Baker. *Actor Systems for Real-Time Computation* MIT EECS Doctoral Dissertation. January 1978.
- Michael Smyth. *Power domains* Journal of Computer and System Sciences. 1978.
- George Milne and Robin Milner. *Concurrent processes and their syntax* JACM. April, 1979.
- Nissim Francez, C.A.R. Hoare, Daniel Lehmann, and Willem-Paul de Roever. *Semantics of nondeterminism, concurrency, and communication* Journal of Computer and System Sciences. December 1979.
- Nancy Lynch and Michael J. Fischer. *On describing the behavior of distributed systems* in Semantics of Concurrent Computation. Springer-Verlag. 1979.
- Jerald Schwartz *Denotational semantics of parallelism* in Semantics of Concurrent Computation. Springer-Verlag. 1979.
- William Wadge. *An extensional treatment of dataflow deadlock* Semantics of Concurrent Computation. Springer-Verlag. 1979.
- Ralph-Johan Back. *Semantics of Unbounded Nondeterminism* ICALP 1980.
- David Park. *On the semantics of fair parallelism* Proceedings of the Winter School on Formal Software Specification. Springer-Verlag. 1980.
- Will Clinger, *of Actor Semantics* (http://hdl.handle.net/1721.1/6935"Foundations). *MIT Mathematics Doctoral Dissertation, June 1981.*
- Lloyd Allison, *A Practical Introduction to Denotational Semantics* Cambridge University Press. 1987.

- P. America, J. de Bakker, J. N. Kok and J. Rutten. *Denotational semantics of a parallel object-oriented language* Information and Computation, 83(2):152–205 (1989)
- David A. Schmidt, *The Structure of Typed Programming Languages*. MIT Press, Cambridge, Massachusetts, 1994. ISBN 0-262-69171-X.
- M. Korff *True concurrency semantics for single pushout graph transformations with applications to actor systems* Working papers of the Int. Workshop on Information Systems - Correctness and Reusability. World Scientific. 1995.
- M. Korff and L. Ribeiro *Concurrent derivations as single pushout graph grammar processes* Proceedings of the Joint COMPUGRAPH/SEMAGRAPH Workshop on Graph Rewriting and Computation. ENTCS Vol 2, Elsevier. 1995.
- Thati, Prasanna, Carolyn Talcott, and Gul Agha. *Techniques for Executing and Reasoning About Specification Diagrams* International Conference on Algebraic Methodology and Software Technology (AMAST), 2004.
- J.C.M. Baeten, T. Basten, and M.A. Reniers. *Algebra of Communicating Processes* Cambridge University Press. 2005.
- He Jifeng and C.A.R. Hoare. *Linking Theories of Concurrency* United Nations University International Institute for Software Technology UNU-IIST Report No. 328. July, 2005.
- Luca Aceto and Andrew D. Gordon (editors). *Algebraic Process Calculi: The First Twenty Five Years and Beyond* Process Algebra. Bertinoro, Forlì, Italy, August 1–5, 2005.
- A. W. Roscoe. *The Theory and Practice of Concurrency*, Prentice Hall, ISBN 0-13-674409-5. Revised 2005.


## External links


- *Denotational Semantics* (http://www.csse.monash.edu.au/~lloyd/tilde/Semantics/). Overview of book by Lloyd Allison
- *Structure of Programming Languages I: Denotational Semantics* (http://www.risc.uni-linz.ac.at/people/schreine/courses/densem/densem.html). Course notes from 1995 by Wolfgang Schreiner

# Domain_theory

**Domain theory** is a branch of mathematics that studies special kinds of partially ordered sets (posets) commonly called **domains**. Consequently, domain theory can be considered as a branch of order theory. The field has major applications in computer science, where it is used to specify denotational semantics, especially for functional programming languages. Domain theory formalizes the intuitive ideas of approximation and convergence in a very general way and has close relations to topology. An alternative important approach to denotational semantics in computer science is that of metric spaces.

## Motivation and intuition

The primary motivation for the study of domains, which was initiated by Dana Scott in the late 1960s, was the search for a denotational semantics of the lambda calculus. In this formalism, one considers "functions" specified by certain terms in the language. In a purely syntactic way, one can go from simple functions to functions that take other functions as their input arguments. Using again just the syntactic transformations available in this formalism, one can obtain so called fixed point combinators (the best-known of which is the Y combinator); these, by definition, have the property that $f(\mathbf{Y}(f)) = \mathbf{Y}(f)$ for all functions $f$.

To formulate such a denotational semantics, one might first try to construct a *model* for the lambda calculus, in which a genuine (total) function is associated with each lambda term. Such a model would formalize a link between the lambda calculus as a purely syntactic system and the lambda calculus as a notational system for manipulating concrete mathematical functions. The Combinator calculus is such a model. However, the elements of the Combinator calculus are functions from functions to functions; in order for the elements of a model of the lambda calculus to be of arbitrary domain and range, they could not be true functions, only partial functions.

Scott got around this difficulty by formalizing a notion of "partial" or "incomplete" information to represent computations that have not yet returned a result. This was modeled by considering, for each domain of computation (e.g. the natural numbers), an additional element that represents an *undefined* output, i.e. the "result" of a computation that never ends. In addition, the domain of computation is equipped with an *ordering relation*, in which the "undefined result" is the least element.

The important step to find a model for the lambda calculus is to consider only those functions (on such a partially ordered set) which are guaranteed to have least fixed points. The set of these functions, together with an appropriate ordering, is again a "domain" in the sense of the theory. But the restriction to a subset of all available functions has another great benefit: it is possible to obtain domains that contain their own function spaces, i.e. one gets functions that can be applied to themselves.

Beside these desirable properties, domain theory also allows for an appealing intuitive interpretation. As mentioned above, the domains of computation are always partially ordered. This ordering represents a hierarchy of information or knowledge. The higher an element is within the order, the more specific it is and the more information it contains. Lower elements represent incomplete knowledge or intermediate results.

Computation then is modeled by applying monotone functions repeatedly on elements of the domain in order to refine a result. Reaching a fixed point is equivalent to finishing a calculation. Domains provide a superior setting for these ideas since fixed points of monotone functions can be guaranteed to exist and, under additional restrictions, can be approximated from below.

# A guide to the formal definitions

In this section, the central concepts and definitions of domain theory will be introduced. The above intuition of domains being *information orderings* will be emphasized to motivate the mathematical formalization of the theory. The precise formal definitions are to be found in the dedicated articles for each concept. A list of general order-theoretic definitions which include domain theoretic notions as well can be found in the order theory glossary. The most important concepts of domain theory will nonetheless be introduced below.

## Directed sets as converging specifications

As mentioned before, domain theory deals with partially ordered sets to model a domain of computation. The goal is to interpret the elements of such an order as *pieces of information* or *(partial) results of a computation*, where elements that are higher in the order extend the information of the elements below them in a consistent way. From this simple intuition it is already clear that domains often do not have a greatest element, since this would mean that there is an element that contains the information of *all* other elements - a rather uninteresting situation.

A concept that plays an important role in the theory is the one of a **directed subset** of a domain, i.e. of a non-empty subset of the order in which each two elements have some upper bound that is an element of this subset. In view of our intuition about domains, this means that every two pieces of information within the directed subset are *consistently* extended by some other element in the subset. Hence we can view directed sets as *consistent specifications*, i.e. as sets of partial results in which no two elements are contradictory. This interpretation can be compared with the notion of a convergent sequence in analysis, where each element is more specific than the preceding one. Indeed, in the theory of metric spaces, sequences play a role that is in many aspects analogous to the role of directed sets in domain theory.

Now, as in the case of sequences, we are interested in the *limit* of a directed set. According to what was said above, this would be an element that is the most general piece of information which extends the information of all elements of the directed set, i.e. the unique element that contains *exactly* the information that was present in the directed set - and nothing more. In the formalization of order theory, this is just the **least upper bound** of the directed set. As in the case of limits of sequences, least upper bounds of directed sets do not always exist.

Naturally, one has a special interest in those domains of computations in which all consistent specifications *converge*, i.e. in orders in which all directed sets have a least upper bound. This property defines the class of **directed complete partial orders**, or **dcpo** for short. Indeed, most considerations of domain theory do only consider orders that are at least directed complete.

From the underlying idea of partially specified results as representing incomplete knowledge, one derives another desirable property: the existence of a **least element**. Such an element models that state of no information - the place where most computations start. It also can be regarded as the output of a computation that does not return any result at all.

## Computations and domains

Now that we have some basic formal descriptions of what a domain of computation should be, we can turn to the computations themselves. Clearly, these have to be functions, taking inputs from some computational domain and returning outputs in some (possibly different) domain. However, one would also expect that the output of a function will contain more information when the information content of the input is increased. Formally, this means that we want a function to be **monotonic**.

When dealing with **dcpos**, one might also want computations to be compatible with the formation of limits of a directed set. Formally, this means that, for some function $f$, the image $f(D)$ of a directed set $D$ (i.e. the set of the images of each element of $D$) is again directed and has as a least upper bound the image of the least upper bound of $D$. One could also say that $f$ *preserves directed suprema*. Also note that, by considering directed sets of two elements, such a function also has to be monotonic. These properties give rise to the notion of a **Scott-continuous** function. Since this often is not ambiguous one also may speak of *continuous functions*.

## Approximation and finiteness

Domain theory is a purely *qualitative* approach to modeling the structure of information states. One can say that something contains more information, but the amount of additional information is not specified. Yet, there are some situations in which one wants to speak about elements that are in a sense much simpler (or much more incomplete) than a given state of information. For example, in the natural subset-inclusion ordering on some powerset, any infinite element (i.e. set) is much more "informative" than any of its *finite* subsets.

If one wants to model such a relationship, one may first want to consider the induced strict order $<$ of a domain with order $\leq$. However, while this is a useful notion in the case of total orders, it does not tell us much in the case of partially ordered sets. Considering again inclusion-orders of sets, a set is already strictly smaller than another, possibly infinite, set if it contains just one less element. One would, however, hardly agree that this captures the notion of being "much simpler".

## Way-below relation

A more elaborate approach leads to the definition of the so-called **order of approximation**, which is more suggestively also called the **way-below relation**. An element $x$ is *way below* an element $y$, if, for every directed set $D$ with supremum such that

$$,$$

there is some element $d$ in $D$ such that

$$.$$

Then one also says that $x$ *approximates* $y$ and writes

$$.$$

This does imply that

$$,$$

since the singleton set $\{y\}$ is directed. For an example, in an ordering of sets, an infinite set is way above any of its finite subsets. On the other hand, consider the directed set (in fact: the chain) of finite sets

Since the supremum of this chain is the set of all natural numbers $\mathbf{N}$, this shows that no infinite set is way below $\mathbf{N}$.

However, being way below some element is a *relative* notion and does not reveal much about an element alone. For example, one would like to characterize finite sets in an order-theoretic way, but even infinite sets can be way below some other set. The special property of these **finite** elements $x$ is that they are way below themselves, i.e.

$$.$$

An element with this property is also called **compact**. Yet, such elements do not have to be "finite" nor "compact" in any other mathematical usage of the terms. The notation is nonetheless motivated by certain parallels to the respective notions in set theory and topology. The compact elements of a domain have the important special property that they cannot be obtained as a limit of a directed set in which they did not already occur.

Many other important results about the way-below relation support the claim that this definition is appropriate to capture many important aspects of a domain.

## Bases of domains

The previous thoughts raise another question: is it possible to guarantee that all elements of a domain can be obtained as a limit of much simpler elements? This is quite relevant in practice, since we cannot compute infinite objects but we may still hope to approximate them arbitrarily closely.

More generally, we would like to restrict to a certain subset of elements as being sufficient for getting all other elements as least upper bounds. Hence, one defines a **base** of a poset $P$ as being a subset $B$ of $P$, such that, for each $x$ in $P$, the set of elements in $B$ that are way below $x$ contains a directed set with supremum $x$. The poset $P$ is a *continuous poset* if it has some base. Especially, $P$ itself is a base in this situation. In many applications, one restricts to continuous (d)cpos as a main object of study.

Finally, an even stronger restriction on a partially ordered set is given by requiring the existence of a base of *compact* elements. Such a poset is called **algebraic**. From the viewpoint of denotational semantics, algebraic posets are particularly well-behaved, since they allow for the approximation of all elements even when restricting to finite ones. As remarked before, not every finite element is "finite" in a classical sense and it may well be that the finite elements constitute an uncountable set.

In some cases, however, the base for a poset is countable. In this case, one speaks of an **ω-continuous** poset. Accordingly, if the countable base consists entirely of finite elements, we obtain an order that is **ω-algebraic**.

## Special types of domains

A simple special case of a domain is known as an **elementary** or **flat domain**. This consists of a set of incomparable elements, such as the integers, along with a single "bottom" element considered smaller than all other elements.

One can obtain a number of other interesting special classes of ordered structures that could be suitable as "domains". We already mentioned continuous posets and algebraic posets. More special versions of both are continuous and algebraic cpos. Adding even further completeness properties one obtains continuous lattices and algebraic lattices, which are just complete lattices with the respective properties. For the algebraic case, one finds broader classes of posets which are still worth studying: historically, the Scott domains were the first structures to be studied in domain theory. Still wider classes of domains are constituted by SFP-domains, L-domains, and bifinite domains.

All of these classes of orders can be cast into various categories of dcpos, using functions which are monotone, Scott-continuous, or even more specialized as morphisms. Finally, note that the term *domain* itself is not exact and thus is only used as an abbreviation when a formal definition has been given before or when the details are irrelevant.

## Important results

A poset $D$ is a dcpo if and only if each chain in $D$ has a supremum.

If $f$ is a continuous function on a poset $D$ then it has a least fixed point, given as the least upper bound of all finite iterations of $f$ on the least element 0: $V_{n \text{ in } \mathbf{N}} f^n(0)$. This is the Kleene fixed-point theorem.

## Generalizations

- Synthetic domain theory [1]
- Topological domain theory [2]
- A continuity space is a generalization of metric spaces and posets, that can be used to unify the notions of metric spaces and domains.

## See also

- Scott domain
- Scott information system
- Type theory
- Category theory

## Further reading

- G. Gierz, K. H. Hofmann, K. Keimel, J. D. Lawson, M. Mislove, and D. S. Scott (2003). "Continuous Lattices and Domains". *Encyclopedia of Mathematics and its Applications*. **93**. Cambridge University Press. ISBN 0-521-80338-1.
- S. Abramsky, A. Jung (1994). "Domain theory" [3]. In S. Abramsky, D. M. Gabbay, T. S. E. Maibaum, editors, (PDF). *Handbook of Logic in Computer Science*. **III**. Oxford University Press. ISBN 0-19-853762-X. Retrieved 2007-10-13.
- Alex Simpson (2001-2002). "Part III: Topological Spaces from a Computational Perspective" [4]. *Mathematical Structures for Semantics*. Retrieved 2007-10-13.
- D. S. Scott (1975). "Data types as lattices". *Proceedings of the International Summer Institute and Logic Colloquium, Kiel*, in *Lecture Notes in Mathematics* (Springer-Verlag) **499**: 579–651.
- Carl A. Gunter (1992). *Semantics of Programming Languages*. MIT Press.
- B. A. Davey and H. A. Priestley (2002). *Introduction to Lattices and Order* (2nd ed.). Cambridge University Press. ISBN 0-521-78451-4.
- Carl Hewitt and Henry Baker (August 1977). "Actors and Continuous Functionals". *Proceedings of IFIP Working Conference on Formal Description of Programming Concepts*.

## External links

- Introduction to Domain Theory [5] by Graham Hutton, University of Nottingham

## References


[1] http://citeseerx.ist.psu.edu/viewdoc/download?doi=10.1.1.55.903&rep=rep1&type=pdf
[2] http://homepages.inf.ed.ac.uk/als/Research/topological-domain-theory.html
[3] http://www.cs.bham.ac.uk/~axj/pub/papers/handy1.pdf
[4] http://www.dcs.ed.ac.uk/home/als/Teaching/MSfS/l3.ps
[5] http://www.cs.nott.ac.uk/~gmh/domains.html

# Actor_model

In computer science, the **Actor model** is a mathematical model of concurrent computation that treats "actors" as the universal primitives of concurrent digital computation: in response to a message that it receives, an actor can make local decisions, create more actors, send more messages, and determine how to respond to the next message received. The Actor model originated in 1973.[1] It has been used both as a framework for a theoretical understanding of computation, and as the theoretical basis for several practical implementations of concurrent systems. The relationship of the model to other work is discussed in Indeterminacy in concurrent computation and Actor model and process calculi.

## History

According to Carl Hewitt, unlike previous models of computation, the Actor model was inspired by physics including general relativity and quantum mechanics.[2] It was also influenced by the programming languages Lisp, Simula and early versions of Smalltalk, as well as capability-based systems and packet switching. Its development was "motivated by the prospect of highly parallel computing machines consisting of dozens, hundreds or even thousands of independent microprocessors, each with its own local memory and communications processor, communicating via a high-performance communications network."[3] Since that time, the advent of massive concurrency through multi-core computer architectures has revived interest in the Actor model.

Following Hewitt, Bishop, and Steiger's 1973 publication, Irene Greif developed an operational semantics for the Actors model as part of her doctoral research.[4] Two years later, Henry Baker and Hewitt published a set of axiomatic laws for Actor systems.[5] Other major milestones include William Clinger's dissertation, in 1981, introducing a denotational semantics based on power domains,[3] and Gul Agha's 1985 dissertation which further developed a transition-based semantic model complementary to Clinger's.[6] This resulted in the full development of actor model theory.

Major software implementation work was done by Russ Atkinson, Beppe Attardi, Henry Baker, Gerry Barber, Peter Bishop, Peter de Jong, Ken Kahn, Henry Lieberman, Carl Manning, Tom Reinhardt, Richard Steiger, and Dan Theriault, in the Message Passing Semantics Group at Massachusetts Institute of Technology (MIT). Research groups led by Chuck Seitz at California Institute of Technology (Caltech) and Bill Dally at MIT constructed computer architectures that further developed the message passing in the model. See Actor model implementation.

Research on the Actor model has been carried out at Caltech Computer Science, Kyoto University Tokoro Laboratory, MCC, MIT Artificial Intelligence Laboratory, SRI, Stanford University, University of Illinois at Urbana-Champaign Open Systems Laboratory [7], Pierre and Marie Curie University (University of Paris 6), University of Pisa, University of Tokyo Yonezawa Laboratory and elsewhere.

## Fundamental concepts

The Actor model adopts the philosophy that *everything is an actor*. This is similar to the *everything is an object* philosophy used by some object-oriented programming languages, but differs in that object-oriented software is typically executed sequentially, while the Actor model is inherently concurrent.

An actor is a computational entity that, in response to a message it receives, can concurrently:

- send a finite number of messages to other actors;
- create a finite number of new actors;
- designate the behavior to be used for the next message it receives.

There is no assumed sequence to the above actions and they could be carried out in parallel.

Decoupling the sender from communications sent was a fundamental advance of the Actor model enabling asynchronous communication and control structures as patterns of passing messages.[8]

Recipients of messages are identified by address, sometimes called "mailing address". Thus an actor can only communicate with actors whose addresses it has. It can obtain those from a message it receives, or if the address is for an actor it has itself created.

The Actor model is characterized by inherent concurrency of computation within and among actors, dynamic creation of actors, inclusion of actor addresses in messages, and interaction only through direct asynchronous message passing with no restriction on message arrival order.

## Formal systems

Over the years, several different formal systems have been developed which permit reasoning about systems in the Actor model. These include:

- Operational semantics[4] [9]
- Laws for Actor systems[5]
- Denotational semantics[3] [10]
- Transition semantics[6]

There are also formalisms that are not fully faithful to the Actor model in that they do not formalize the guaranteed delivery of messages including the following (See Attempts to relate Actor semantics to algebra and linear logic):

- Several different Actor algebras[11] [12] [13]
- Linear logic[14]

## Applications

The Actors model can be used as a framework for modelling, understanding, and reasoning about, a wide range of concurrent systems. For example:

- Electronic mail (e-mail) can be modeled as an Actor system. Accounts are modeled as Actors and email addresses as Actor addresses.
- Web Services can be modeled with SOAP endpoints modeled as Actor addresses.
- Objects with locks (*e.g.* as in Java and C#) can be modeled as a **Serializer**, provided that their implementations are such that messages can continually arrive (perhaps by being stored in an internal queue). A serializer is an important kind of Actor defined by the property that it is continually available to the arrival of new messages; every message sent to a serializer is guaranteed to arrive.
- Testing and Test Control Notation (TTCN), both TTCN-2 and TTCN-3, follows Actor model rather closely. In TTCN, Actor is a test component: either parallel test component (PTC) or main test component (MTC). Test components can send and receive messages to and from remote partners (peer test components or test system interface), the latter being identified by its address. Each test component has a behaviour tree bound to it; test components run in parallel and can be dynamically created by parent test components. Built-in language constructs allow the definition of actions to be taken when an expected message is received from the internal message queue, like sending a message to another peer entity or creating new test components.

# Message-passing semantics

The Actor model is about the semantics of message passing.

## Unbounded nondeterminism controversy

Arguably, the first concurrent programs were interrupt handlers. During the course of its normal operation, a computer needed to be able to receive information from outside (characters from a keyboard, packets from a network, *etc.*). So when the information arrived, execution of the computer was "interrupted" and special code called an interrupt handler was called to *put* the information in a buffer where it could be subsequently retrieved.

In the early 1960s, interrupts began to be used to simulate the concurrent execution of several programs on a single processor.[15] Having concurrency with shared memory gave rise to the problem of concurrency control. Originally, this problem was conceived as being one of mutual exclusion on a single computer. Edsger Dijkstra developed semaphores and later, between 1971 and 1973,[16] Tony Hoare[17] and Per Brinch Hansen[18] developed monitors to solve the mutual exclusion problem. However, neither of these solutions provided a programming-language construct that encapsulated access to shared resources. This encapsulation was later accomplished by the serializer construct ([Hewitt and Atkinson 1977, 1979] and [Atkinson 1980]).

The first models of computation (*e.g.* Turing machines, Post productions, the lambda calculus, *etc.*) were based on mathematics and made use of a global state to represent a computational *step* (later generalized in [McCarthy and Hayes 1969] and [Dijkstra 1976] see Event orderings versus global state). Each computational step was from one global state of the computation to the next global state. The global state approach was continued in automata theory for finite state machines and push down stack machines, including their nondeterministic versions. Such nondeterministic automata have the property of bounded nondeterminism; that is, if a machine always halts when started in its initial state, then there is a bound on the number of states in which it halts.

Edsger Dijkstra further developed the nondeterministic global state approach. Dijkstra's model gave rise to a controversy concerning *unbounded nondeterminism*. Unbounded nondeterminism (also called *unbounded indeterminacy*), is a property of concurrency by which the amount of delay in servicing a request can become unbounded as a result of arbitration of contention for shared resources *while still guaranteeing that the request will eventually be serviced*. Hewitt argued that the Actor model should provide the guarantee of service. In Dijkstra's model, although there could be an unbounded amount of time between the execution of sequential instructions on a computer, a (parallel) program that started out in a well defined state could terminate in only a bounded number of states [Dijkstra 1976]. Consequently, his model could not provide the guarantee of service. Dijkstra argued that it was impossible to implement unbounded nondeterminism.

Hewitt argued otherwise: there is no bound that can be placed on how long it takes a computational circuit called an *arbiter* to settle (see metastability in electronics). Arbiters are used in computers to deal with the circumstance that computer clocks operate asynchronously with input from outside, *e.g.* keyboard input, disk access, network input, *etc.* So it could take an unbounded time for a message sent to a computer to be received and in the meantime the computer could traverse an unbounded number of states.

The Actor Model features unbounded nondeterminism which was captured in a mathematical model by Will Clinger using domain theory.[3] There is no global state in the Actor model.

## Direct communication and asynchrony

Messages in the Actor model are not necessarily buffered. This was a sharp break with previous approaches to models of concurrent computation. The lack of buffering caused a great deal of misunderstanding at the time of the development of the Actor model and is still a controversial issue. Some researchers argued that the messages are buffered in the "ether" or the "environment". Also, messages in the Actor model are simply sent (like packets in IP); there is no requirement for a synchronous handshake with the recipient.

## Actor creation plus addresses in messages means variable topology

A natural development of the Actor model was to allow addresses in messages. Influenced by packet switched networks [1961 and 1964], Hewitt proposed the development of a new model of concurrent computation in which communications would not have any required fields at all: they could be empty. Of course, if the sender of a communication desired a recipient to have access to addresses which the recipient did not already have, the address would have to be sent in the communication.

A computation might need to send a message to a recipient from which it would later receive a response. The way to do this is to send a communication which has the message along with the address of another actor called the *resumption* (sometimes also called continuation or stack frame) along with the message. The recipient could then cause a response message to be sent to the resumption.

Actor creation plus the inclusion of the addresses of actors in messages means that Actors have a potentially variable topology in their relationship to one another much as the objects in Simula also had a variable topology in their relationship to one another.

## Inherently concurrent

As opposed to the previous approach based on composing sequential processes, the Actor model was developed as an inherently concurrent model. In the Actor model sequentiality was a special case that derived from concurrent computation as explained in Actor model theory.

## No requirement on order of message arrival

Hewitt argued against adding the requirement that messages must arrive in the order in which they are sent to the Actor. If output message ordering is desired, then it can be modeled by a queue Actor that provides this functionality. Such a queue Actor would queue the messages that arrived so that they could be retrieved in FIFO order. So if an Actor X  sent a message M1  to an Actor Y, and later X  sent another message M2  to Y, there is no requirement that M1  arrives at Y  before M2.

In this respect the Actor model mirrors packet switching systems which do not guarantee that packets must be received in the order sent. Not providing the order of delivery guarantee allows packet switching to buffer packets, use multiple paths to send packets, resend damaged packets, and to provide other optimizations.

For example, Actors are allowed to pipeline the processing of messages. What this means is that in the course of processing a message M1, an Actor can designate the behavior to be used to process the next message, and then in fact begin processing another message M2  before it has finished processing M1. Just because an Actor is allowed to pipeline the processing of messages does not mean that it *must* pipeline the processing. Whether a message is pipelined is an engineering tradeoff. How would an external observer know whether the processing of a message by an Actor has been pipelined? There is no ambiguity in the definition of an Actor created by the possibility of pipelining. Of course, it is possible to perform the pipeline optimization incorrectly in some implementations, in which case unexpected behavior may occur.

## Locality

Another important characteristic of the Actor model is locality.

Locality means that in processing a message an Actor can send messages only to addresses that it receives in the message, addresses that it already had before it received the message and addresses for Actors that it creates while processing the message. (But see Synthesizing Addresses of Actors.)

Also locality means that there is no simultaneous change in multiple locations. In this way it differs from some other models of concurrency, *e.g.*, the Petri net model in which tokens are simultaneously removed from multiple locations and placed in other locations.

## Composing Actor Systems

The idea of composing Actor systems into larger ones is an important aspect of modularity that was developed in Gul Agha's doctoral dissertation,[6] developed later by Gul Agha, Ian Mason, Scott Smith, and Carolyn Talcott.[9]

## Behaviors

A key innovation was the introduction of *behavior* specified as a mathematical function to express what an Actor does when it processes a message including specifying a new behavior to process the next message that arrives. Behaviors provided a mechanism to mathematically model the sharing in concurrency.

Behaviors also freed the Actor model from implementation details, *e.g.*, the Smalltalk-72 token stream interpreter. However, it is critical to understand that the efficient implementation of systems described by the Actor model require *extensive* optimization. See Actor model implementation for details.

## Modeling other concurrency systems

Other concurrency systems (*e.g.* process calculi) can be modeled in the Actor model using a two-phase commit protocol.[19]

## Computational Representation Theorem

There is a *Computational Representation Theorem* in the Actor model for systems which are closed in the sense that they do not receive communications from outside. The mathematical denotation denoted by a closed system $S$ is constructed from an initial behavior $\perp_S$ and a behavior-approximating function $\textbf{progression}_S$. These obtain increasingly better approximations and construct a denotation (meaning) for $S$ as follows [Hewitt 2008; Clinger 1981]:

$$\textbf{Denote}_S \equiv \sqcup_{i \in \omega} \textbf{progression}_S^{\ i}(\perp_S)$$

In this way, $S$ can be mathematically characterized in terms of all its possible behaviors (including those involving unbounded nondeterminism). Although $\textbf{Denote}_S$ is not an implementation of $S$, it can be used to prove a generalization of the Church-Turing-Rosser-Kleene thesis [Kleene 1943]:

A consequence of the above theorem is that a finite Actor can nondeterministically respond with an uncountable number of different outputs.

## Relationship to mathematical logic

The development of the Actor model has an interesting relationship to mathematical logic. One of the key motivations for its development was to understand and deal with the control structure issues that arose in development of the Planner programming language. Once the Actor model was initially defined, an important challenge was to understand the power of the model relative to Robert Kowalski's thesis that "computation can be subsumed by deduction". Kowalski's thesis turned out to be false for the concurrent computation in the Actor model (see Indeterminacy in concurrent computation). This result is still somewhat controversial and it reversed previous expectations because Kowalski's thesis is true for sequential computation and even some kinds of parallel computation, *e.g.* the lambda calculus.

Nevertheless attempts were made to extend logic programming to concurrent computation. However, Hewitt and Agha [1991] claimed that the resulting systems were not deductive in the following sense: computational steps of the concurrent logic programming systems do not follow deductively from previous steps (see Indeterminacy in concurrent computation).

## Migration

Migration in the Actor model is the ability of Actors to change locations. *E.g.*, in his dissertation, Aki Yonezawa modeled a post office that customer Actors could enter, change locations within while operating, and exit. An Actor that can migrate can be modeled by having a location Actor that changes when the Actor migrates. However the faithfulness of this modeling is controversial and the subject of research.

## Security

The security of Actors can be protected in the following ways:

- hardwiring in which Actors are physically connected
- computer hardware as in Burroughs B5000, Lisp machine, *etc.*
- virtual machines as in Java virtual machine, Common Language Runtime, *etc.*
- operating systems as in capability-based systems
- signing and/or encryption of Actors and their addresses

## Synthesizing addresses of actors

A delicate point in the Actor model is the ability to synthesize the address of an Actor. In some cases security can be used to prevent the synthesis of addresses (see Security). However, if an Actor address is simply a bit string then clearly it can be synthesized although it may be difficult or even infeasible to guess the address of an Actor if the bit strings are long enough. SOAP uses a URL for the address of an endpoint where an Actor can be reached. Since a URL is a character string, it can clearly be synthesized although encryption can make it virtually impossible to guess.

Synthesizing the addresses of Actors is usually modeled using mapping. The idea is to use an Actor system to perform the mapping to the actual Actor addresses. For example, on a computer the memory structure of the computer can be modeled as an Actor system that does the mapping. In the case of SOAP addresses, it's modeling the DNS and rest of the URL mapping.

## Contrast with other models of message-passing concurrency

Robin Milner's initial published work on concurrency[20] was also notable in that it was not based on composing sequential processes. His work differed from the Actor model because it was based on a fixed number of processes of fixed topology communicating numbers and strings using synchronous communication. The original Communicating Sequential Processes model[21] published by Tony Hoare differed from the Actor model because it was based on the parallel composition of a fixed number of sequential processes connected in a fixed topology, and communicating using synchronous message-passing based on process names (see Actor model and process calculi history). Later versions of CSP abandoned communication based on process names in favor of anonymous communication via channels, an approach also used in Milner's work on the Calculus of Communicating Systems and the $\pi$-calculus.

These early models by Milner and Hoare both had the property of bounded nondeterminism. Modern, theoretical CSP ([Hoare 1985] and [Roscoe 2005]) explicitly provides unbounded nondeterminism.

# Influence

The Actor Model has been influential on both theory development and practical software development.

## Theory

The Actor Model has influenced the development of the Pi-calculus and subsequent Process calculi. In his Turing lecture, Robin Milner wrote:[22]

> *Now, the pure lambda-calculus is built with just two kinds of thing: terms and variables. Can we achieve the same economy for a process calculus? Carl Hewitt, with his Actors model, responded to this challenge long ago; he declared that a value, an operator on values, and a process should all be the same kind of thing: an Actor.*
>
> *This goal impressed me, because it implies the homogeneity and completeness of expression ... But it was long before I could see how to attain the goal in terms of an algebraic calculus...*
>
> *So, in the spirit of Hewitt, our first step is to demand that all things denoted by terms or accessed by names--values, registers, operators, processes, objects--are all of the same kind of thing; they should all be processes.*

## Practice

The Actor Model has had extensive influence on commercial practice. For example Twitter has used actors for scalability.[23] Also, Microsoft has used the Actor Model in the development of its Asynchronous Agents Library.[24] There are numerous other Actor libraries listed in the Actor Libraries and Frameworks section below.

# Current issues

According to Hewitt [2006], the Actor model faces issues in computer and communications architecture, concurrent programming languages, and Web Services including the following:

- scalability: the challenge of scaling up concurrency both locally and nonlocally.
- transparency: bridging the chasm between local and nonlocal concurrency. Transparency is currently a controversial issue. Some researchers have advocated a strict separation between local concurrency using concurrent programming languages (e.g. Java and C#) from nonlocal concurrency using SOAP for Web services. Strict separation produces a lack of transparency that causes problems when it is desirable/necessary to change between local and nonlocal access to Web Services (see distributed computing).
- inconsistency: Inconsistency is the norm because all very large knowledge systems about human information system interactions are inconsistent. This inconsistency extends to the documentation and specifications of very large systems (e.g. Microsoft Windows software, etc.), which are internally inconsistent.

Many of the ideas introduced in the Actor model are now also finding application in multi-agent systems for these same reasons [Hewitt 2006b 2007b]. The key difference is that agent systems (in most definitions) impose extra constraints upon the Actors, typically requiring that they make use of commitments and goals.

The Actor model is also being applied to client cloud computing.[25]

## Actor researchers

Important contributions to the semantics of Actors have been made by: Gul Agha, Beppe Attardi, Henry Baker, Will Clinger, Irene Greif, Carl Hewitt, Carl Manning, Ian Mason, Ugo Montanari, Maria Simi, Scott Smith, Carolyn Talcott, Prasanna Thati, and Aki Yonezawa.

Important contributions to the implementation of Actors have been made by: Bill Athas, Russ Atkinson, Beppe Attardi, Henry Baker, Gerry Barber, Peter Bishop, Nanette Boden, Jean-Pierre Briot, Bill Dally, Peter de Jong, Jessie Dedecker, Travis Desell, Ken Kahn, Carl Hewitt, Henry Lieberman, Carl Manning, Tom Reinhardt, Chuck Seitz, Richard Steiger, Dan Theriault, Mario Tokoro, Carlos Varela, Darrell Woelk.

## Programming with Actors

A number of different programming languages employ the Actor model or some variation of it. These languages include:

### Early Actor programming languages

- Act 1, 2 and 3[26] [27]
- Acttalk[28]
- Ani[29]
- Cantor[30]
- Rosette[31]

### Later Actor programming languages

- ABCL
- AmbientTalk[32]
- Axum[33]
- D
- E
- Erlang
- Fantom
- Humus[37]
- Io
- Ptolemy Project
- Rebeca Modeling Language
- Reia
- Rust
- SALSA[34]
- Scala[35] [36]
- Scratch

### Actor libraries and frameworks

Actor libraries or frameworks have also been implemented to permit actor-style programming in languages that don't have actors built-in. Among these frameworks are:

| Name | Status | Latest release | License | Languages |
|---|---|---|---|---|
| Akka [38] | Active | 2012-03-06 | Apache 2.0 | Java and Scala |
| Ateji PX [39] | Active | ? | ? | Java |
| F# MailboxProcessor [40] | Active | same as F# (built-in core library) | Apache License | F# |
| Korus [41] | Active | 2010-02-01 | GNU GPL 3 | Java |
| Kilim [42][43] | Active | 2011-10-13[44] | MIT | Java |
| ActorFoundry (based on Kilim) | Active? | 2008-12-28 | ? | Java |
| ActorKit [45] | Active | 2011-02-11[46] | BSD | Objective-C |
| NAct [47] | Active | 2012-02-28 | LGPL 3.0 | .NET |
| Retlang [48] | Active? | 2010-12-01 | New BSD | .NET |
| Jetlang [49] | Active | 2011-11-29 | New BSD | Java |
| Haskell-Actor [50] | Active? | 2008 | New BSD | Haskell |
| GPars [51] (was GParallelizer) | Active | 2011-10-20 | Apache 2.0 | Groovy |
| PARLEY [52] | Active? | 2007-22-07 | GNU GPL 2.1 | Python |
| Pykka [53] (inspired by Akka) | Active | 2011-09-24 | Apache 2.0 | Python |
| Termite Scheme [54] | Active? | 2009 | LGPL | Scheme (Gambit implementation) |
| Theron [55] | Active | 2012-03-31[56] | MIT[57] | C++ |
| Libactor [58] | Active? | 2009 | GPL 2.0 | C |
| Actor-CPP [59] | Active | 2011-12-24[60] | GPL 2.0 | C++ |
| S4 [61] | Active | 2011-11-28[62] | Apache 2.0 | Java |
| libcppa [63] | Active | 2012-01-22[64] | LGPL 3.0 | C++11 |
| Celluloid [65] | Active | 2012-04-02[66] | ? | Ruby |
| LabVIEW Actor Framework [67] | Active | 2012-03-01[68] | ? | LabVIEW |

# See also

- Data flow
- Special relativity (specifically, Relativity of simultaneity) and Quantum physics, for some physical motivation for the Actor model theory
- Multi-agent system
- Neural networks
- Gordon Pask
- Scientific Community Metaphor
- Communicating sequential processes

# References


[1] Carl Hewitt; Peter Bishop and Richard Steiger (1973). *A Universal Modular Actor Formalism for Artificial Intelligence*. IJCAI.

[2] Actor Model of Computation: Scalable Robust Information Systems (http://arxiv.org/pdf/1008.1459v23.pdf), Carl Hewitt, 2011

[3] William Clinger (June 1981). *Foundations of Actor Semantics* (https://dspace.mit.edu/handle/1721.1/6935). Mathematics Doctoral Dissertation. MIT. .

[4] Irene Greif (August 1975). *Semantics of Communicating Parallel Processes*. EECS Doctoral Dissertation. MIT.

[5] Henry Baker; Carl Hewitt (August 1977). *Laws for Communicating Parallel Processes*. IFIP.

[6] Gul Agha (1986). *Actors: A Model of Concurrent Computation in Distributed Systems* (https://dspace.mit.edu/handle/1721.1/6952). Doctoral Dissertation. MIT Press. .

[7] http://osl.cs.uiuc.edu

[8] Carl Hewitt. *Viewing Control Structures as Patterns of Passing Messages* Journal of Artificial Intelligence. June 1977.

[9] Gul Agha; Ian Mason, Scott Smith, and Carolyn Talcott (January 1993). "A Foundation for Actor Computation". *Journal of Functional Programming*.

[10] Carl Hewitt (2006-04-27) (PDF). *What is Commitment? Physical, Organizational, and Social* (http://www.pcs.usp.br/~coin-aamas06/10_commitment-43_16pages.pdf). COIN@AAMAS. .

[11] Mauro Gaspari; Gianluigi Zavattaro (May 1997). *An Algebra of Actors*. Technical Report UBLCS-97-4. University of Bologna.

[12] M. Gaspari; G. Zavattaro (1999). *An Algebra of Actors*. Formal Methods for Open Object Based Systems.

[13] Gul Agha; Prasanna Thati (2004) (PDF). *An Algebraic Theory of Actors and Its Application to a Simple Object-Based Language* (http://formal.cs.uiuc.edu/papers/ATactors_festschrift.pdf). From OO to FM (Dahl Festschrift) LNCS 2635. .

[14] John Darlington; Y. K. Guo (1994). *Formalizing Actors in Linear Logic*. International Conference on Object-Oriented Information Systems.

[15] Brinch-Hansen, Per (2002). *The Origins of Concurrent Programming: From Semaphores to Remote Procedure Calls*. Springer. ISBN 978-0-387-95401-1.

[16] Per Brinch Hansen, *Monitors and Concurrent Pascal: A Personal History*, Comm. ACM 1996, pp 121-172

[17] C.A.R. Hoare, *Monitors: An Operating System Structuring Concept*, Comm. ACM Vol. 17, No. 10. October 1974, pp. 549-557

[18] Brinch Hansen, P., *Operating System Principles*, Prentice-Hall, July 1973.

[19] Frederick Knabe. A Distributed Protocol for Channel-Based Communication with Choice PARLE 1992.

[20] Robin Milner. Processes: A Mathematical Model of Computing Agents in Logic Colloquium 1973.

[21] C.A.R. Hoare. Communicating sequential processes (http://portal.acm.org/citation.cfm?id=359585&dl=GUIDE&coll=GUIDE&CFID=19884966&CFTOKEN=55490895) CACM. August 1978.

[22] "Elements of Interaction" CACM Jam. 1993 (https://dl.acm.org/citation.cfm?id=151240)

[23] "How Twitter is Scaling" (https://waimingmok.wordpress.com/2009/06/27/how-twitter-is-scaling/) retrieved August 29, 2011.

[24] "Actor-Based Programming with the Asynchronous Agents Library" MSDN September 2010.

[25] Carl Hewitt (September/October 2008). "ORGs for Scalable, Robust, Privacy-Friendly Client Cloud Computing". *IEEE Internet Computing* **12** (5).

[26] Henry Lieberman (June 1981). *A Preview of Act 1* (ftp://publications.ai.mit.edu/ai-publications/pdf/AIM-625.pdf). MIT AI memo 625.

[27] Henry Lieberman (June 1981). *Thinking About Lots of Things at Once without Getting Confused: Parallelism in Act 1* (ftp://publications.ai.mit.edu/ai-publications/pdf/AIM-626.pdf). MIT AI memo 626. .

[28] Jean-Pierre Briot. Acttalk: A framework for object-oriented concurrent programming-design and experience 2nd France-Japan workshop. 1999.

[29] Ken Kahn. A Computational Theory of Animation MIT EECS Doctoral Dissertation. August 1979.

[30] William Athas and Nanette Boden Cantor: An Actor Programming System for Scientific Computing in Proceedings of the NSF Workshop on Object-Based Concurrent Programming. 1988. Special Issue of SIGPLAN Notices.

[31] Darrell Woelk. Developing InfoSleuth Agents Using Rosette: An Actor Based Language Proceedings of the CIKM '95 Workshop on Intelligent Information Agents. 1995.

[32]  Dedecker J., Van Cutsem T., Mostinckx S., D'Hondt T., De Meuter W. Ambient-oriented Programming in AmbientTalk. In "Proceedings of the 20th European Conference on Object-Oriented Programming (ECOOP), Dave Thomas (Ed.), Lecture Notes in Computer Science Vol. 4067, pp. 230-254, Springer-Verlag.", 2006

[33]  http://www.eweek.com/c/a/Application-Development/Microsoft-Cooking-Up-New-Parallel-Programming-Language-Axum-868670/

[34]  Carlos Varela and Gul Agha (2001). "Programming Dynamically Reconfigurable Open Systems with SALSA". *ACM SIGPLAN Notices. OOPSLA'2001 Intriguing Technology Track Proceedings* **36**.

[35]  Philipp Haller and Martin Odersky (September 2006) (PDF). *Event-Based Programming without Inversion of Control* (http://lampwww.epfl.ch/~odersky/papers/jmlc06.pdf). Proc. JMLC 2006. .

[36]  Philipp Haller and Martin Odersky (January 2007) (PDF). *Actors that Unify Threads and Events* (http://lamp.epfl.ch/~phaller/doc/haller07coord.pdf). Technical report LAMP 2007. .

[37]  http://www.dalnefre.com/wp/humus/

[38]  http://akka.io

[39]  http://www.ateji.com/px

[40]  http://en.wikibooks.org/wiki/F_Sharp_Programming/MailboxProcessor

[41]  http://code.google.com/p/korus/

[42]  http://kilim.malhar.net/

[43]  Srinivasan, Sriram; Alan Mycroft (2008). "Kilim: Isolation-Typed Actors for Java" (http://www.malhar.net/sriram/kilim/kilim_ecoop08.pdf) (PDF). *European Conference on Object Oriented Programming ECOOP 2008*. Cyprus. . Retrieved 2008-07-24..

[44]  Commits at Github Kilim repository (https://github.com/kilim/kilim/commits/master)

[45]  https://github.com/stevedekorte/ActorKit

[46]  github repository (https://github.com/stevedekorte/ActorKit)

[47]  http://code.google.com/p/n-act/

[48]  http://code.google.com/p/retlang/

[49]  http://code.google.com/p/jetlang/

[50]  http://code.google.com/p/haskellactor/

[51]  http://gpars.codehaus.org/

[52]  http://osl.cs.uiuc.edu/parley/

[53]  http://pykka.readthedocs.org/en/latest/index.html

[54]  http://code.google.com/p/termite/

[55]  http://www.theron-library.com/

[56]  Release 3.04 of Theron (http://www.theron-library.com/index.php?t=story&p=53)

[57]  Theron License (http://www.theron-library.com/index.php?t=page&p=license)

[58]  https://code.google.com/p/libactor/

[59]  http://code.google.com/p/actor-cpp/

[60]  Revision at Google code of Actor-cpp (http://code.google.com/p/actor-cpp/source/list)

[61]  http://s4.io/

[62]  Commits of github s4 repository (https://github.com/s4/s4/commits/master)

[63]  http://libcppa.blogspot.com/

[64]  Commits of github libccpa repository (https://github.com/Neverlord/libcppa/commits/master)

[65]  http://github.com/celluloid/celluloid/

[66]  Release of Celluloid in Rubygems repository (http://rubygems.org/gems/celluloid)

[67]  http://ni.com/actorframework

[68]  Version 3.0.7 of LabVIEW Actor Framework (https://decibel.ni.com/content/docs/DOC-18308)

## Further reading

- Paul Baran. **On Distributed Communications Networks** IEEE Transactions on Communications Systems. March 1964.

- William A. Woods. **Transition network grammars for natural language analysis** CACM. 1970.

- Carl Hewitt. **Procedural Embedding of Knowledge In Planner** IJCAI 1971.

- G.M. Birtwistle, Ole-Johan Dahl, B. Myhrhaug and Kristen Nygaard. **SIMULA Begin** Auerbach Publishers Inc, 1973.

- Carl Hewitt, *et al.* **Actor Induction and Meta-evaluation** Conference Record of ACM Symposium on Principles of Programming Languages, January 1974.

- Carl Hewitt, *et al.* **Behavioral Semantics of Nonrecursive Control Structure** Proceedings of Colloque sur la Programmation, April 1974.

- Irene Greif and Carl Hewitt. **Actor Semantics of PLANNER-73** Conference Record of ACM Symposium on Principles of Programming Languages. January 1975.
- Carl Hewitt. **How to Use What You Know** IJCAI. September, 1975.
- Alan Kay and Adele Goldberg. **Smalltalk-72 Instruction Manual** (http://www.bitsavers.org.nyud.net/pdf/xerox/parc/techReports/Smalltalk-72_Instruction_Manual_Mar76.pdf) Xerox PARC Memo SSL-76-6. May 1976.
- Edsger Dijkstra. **A discipline of programming** Prentice Hall. 1976.
- Carl Hewitt and Henry Baker **Actors and Continuous Functionals** (http://www.lcs.mit.edu/publications/pubs/pdf/MIT-LCS-TR-194.pdf) Proceeding of IFIP Working Conference on Formal Description of Programming Concepts. August 1–5, 1977.
- Carl Hewitt and Russ Atkinson. **Synchronization in Actor Systems** (http://portal.acm.org/citation.cfm?id=512975&coll=portal&dl=ACM) Proceedings of the 4th ACM SIGACT-SIGPLAN symposium on Principles of programming languages. 1977
- Carl Hewitt and Russ Atkinson. **Specification and Proof Techniques for Serializers** IEEE Journal on Software Engineering. January 1979.
- Ken Kahn. **A Computational Theory of Animation** MIT EECS Doctoral Dissertation. August 1979.
- Carl Hewitt, Beppe Attardi, and Henry Lieberman. **Delegation in Message Passing** Proceedings of First International Conference on Distributed Systems Huntsville, AL. October 1979.
- Nissim Francez, C.A.R. Hoare, Daniel Lehmann, and Willem-Paul de Roever. **Semantics of nondetermiism, concurrency, and communication** Journal of Computer and System Sciences. December 1979.
- George Milne and Robin Milner. **Concurrent processes and their syntax** JACM. April 1979.
- Daniel Theriault. **A Primer for the Act-1 Language** MIT AI memo 672. April 1982.
- Daniel Theriault. **Issues in the Design and Implementation of Act 2** MIT AI technical report 728. June 1983.
- Henry Lieberman. **An Object-Oriented Simulator for the Apiary** Conference of the American Association for Artificial Intelligence, Washington, D. C., August 1983
- Carl Hewitt and Peter de Jong. **Analyzing the Roles of Descriptions and Actions in Open Systems** Proceedings of the National Conference on Artificial Intelligence. August 1983.
- Carl Hewitt and Henry Lieberman. **Design Issues in Parallel Architecture for Artificial Intelligence** MIT AI memo 750. Nov. 1983.
- C.A.R. Hoare. **Communicating Sequential Processes** (http://www.usingcsp.com/) Prentice Hall. 1985.
- Carl Hewitt. **The Challenge of Open Systems** Byte Magazine. April 1985. Reprinted in *The foundation of artificial intelligence---a sourcebook* Cambridge University Press. 1990.
- Carl Manning. **Traveler: the actor observatory** ECOOP 1987. Also appears in Lecture Notes in Computer Science, vol. 276.
- William Athas and Charles Seitz **Multicomputers: message-passing concurrent computers** IEEE Computer August 1988.
- William Athas and Nanette Boden **Cantor: An Actor Programming System for Scientific Computing** in Proceedings of the NSF Workshop on Object-Based Concurrent Programming. 1988. Special Issue of SIGPLAN Notices.
- Jean-Pierre Briot. **From objects to actors: Study of a limited symbiosis in Smalltalk-80** Rapport de Recherche 88-58, RXF-LITP, Paris, France, September 1988
- William Dally and Wills, D. **Universal mechanisms for concurrency** PARLE 1989.
- W. Horwat, A. Chien, and W. Dally. **Experience with CST: Programming and Implementation** PLDI. 1989.
- Carl Hewitt. **Towards Open Information Systems Semantics** Proceedings of 10th International Workshop on Distributed Artificial Intelligence. October 23–27, 1990. Bandera, Texas.
- Akinori Yonezawa, Ed. **ABCL: An Object-Oriented Concurrent System** MIT Press. 1990.

- K. Kahn and Vijay A. Saraswat, " Actors as a special case of concurrent constraint (logic) programming (http:// doi.acm.org/10.1145/97946.97955)", in SIGPLAN *Notices*, October 1990. Describes Janus.
- Carl Hewitt. **Open Information Systems Semantics** Journal of Artificial Intelligence. January 1991.
- Carl Hewitt and Jeff Inman. **DAI Betwixt and Between: From "Intelligent Agents" to Open Systems Science** IEEE Transactions on Systems, Man, and Cybernetics. Nov./Dec. 1991.
- Carl Hewitt and Gul Agha. **Guarded Horn clause languages: are they deductive and Logical?** International Conference on Fifth Generation Computer Systems, Ohmsha 1988. Tokyo. Also in *Artificial Intelligence at MIT*, Vol. 2. MIT Press 1991.
- William Dally, *et al.* **The Message-Driven Processor: A Multicomputer Processing Node with Efficient Mechanisms** IEEE Micro. April 1992.
- S. Miriyala, G. Agha, and Y.Sami. **Visulatizing actor programs using predicate transition nets** Journal of Visual Programming. 1992.
- Carl Hewitt and Carl Manning. **Negotiation Architecture for Large-Scale Crisis Management** AAAI-94 Workshop on Models of Conflict Management in Cooperative Problem Solving. Seattle, WA. Aug. 4, 1994.
- Carl Hewitt and Carl Manning. **Synthetic Infrastructures for Multi-Agency Systems** Proceedings of ICMAS '96. Kyoto, Japan. December 8–13, 1996.
- S. Frolund. **Coordinating Distributed Objects: An Actor-Based Approach for Synchronization** MIT Press. November 1996.
- W. Kim. **ThAL: An Actor System for Efficient and Scalable Concurrent Computing** PhD thesis. University of Illinois at Urbana Champaign. 1997.
- Jean-Pierre Briot. **Acttalk: A framework for object-oriented concurrent programming-design and experience** (http://www.ifs.uni-linz.ac.at/~ecoop/cd/papers/ec89/ec890109.pdf) 2nd France-Japan workshop. 1999.
- N. Jamali, P. Thati, and G. Agha. **An actor based architecture for customizing and controlling agent ensembles** IEEE Intelligent Systems. 14(2). 1999.
- Don Box, David Ehnebuske, Gopal Kakivaya, Andrew Layman, Noah Mendelsohn, Henrik Nielsen, Satish Thatte, Dave Winer. **Simple Object Access Protocol (SOAP) 1.1** W3C Note. May 2000.
- M. Astley, D. Sturman, and G. Agha. **Customizable middleware for modular distributed software** CACM. 44(5) 2001.
- Edward Lee, S. Neuendorffer, and M. Wirthlin. **Actor-oriented design of embedded hardware and software systems** (http://ptolemy.eecs.berkeley.edu/papers/02/actorOrientedDesign/newFinal.pdf) Journal of circuits, systems, and computers. 2002.
- P. Thati, R. Ziaei, and G. Agha. **A Theory of May Testing for Actors** Formal Methods for Open Object-based Distributed Systems. March 2002.
- P. Thati, R. Ziaei, and G. Agha. **A theory of may testing for asynchronous calculi with locality and no name matching** Algebraic Methodology and Software Technology. Springer Verlag. September 2002. LNCS 2422.
- Stephen Neuendorffer. **Actor-Oriented Metaprogramming** (http://www.eecs.berkeley.edu/Pubs/TechRpts/ 2005/ERL-05-1.pdf) PhD Thesis. University of California, Berkeley. December, 2004
- Carl Hewitt (2006a) **The repeated demise of logic programming and why it will be reincarnated** What Went Wrong and Why: Lessons from AI Research and Applications. Technical Report SS-06-08. AAAI Press. March 2006.
- Carl Hewitt (2006b) *What is Commitment? Physical, Organizational, and Social* (http://www.pcs.usp.br/ ~coin-aamas06/10_commitment-43_16pages.pdf) COIN@AAMAS. April 27, 2006b.
- Carl Hewitt (2007a) **What is Commitment? Physical, Organizational, and Social (Revised)** Pablo Noriega .et al. editors. LNAI 4386. Springer-Verlag. 2007.
- Carl Hewitt (2007b) **Large-scale Organizational Computing requires Unstratified Paraconsistency and Reflection** COIN@AAMAS'07.

## External links

- Actors on the JVM (http://drdobbs.com//229402193) Dr. Dobb's, April 2011
- A now dated set of speculations by Paul Mackay can be found at *Why has the actor model not succeeded?* (http://www.doc.ic.ac.uk/~nd/surprise_97/journal/vol2/pjm2/)
- JavAct (http://www.irit.fr/PERSONNEL/SMAC/arcangeli/JavAct.html) - a Java library for programming concurrent, distributed, and mobile applications using the actor model (and open implementation principles).
- Functional Java (http://functionaljava.org/) - a Java library of that includes an implementation of concurrent actors with code examples in standard Java and Java 7 BGGA style.
- ActorFoundry (http://osl.cs.uiuc.edu/af) - a Java-based library for Actor programming. The familiar Java syntax, an ant build file and a bunch of example make the entry barrier very low.
- ActiveJava (http://tristan.aubrey-jones.com/code/?project=third_year_project&dir=/) - a prototype Java language extension for Actor programming.
- Akka (http://akka.io) - Actor based library in Scala and Java, from Typesafe.

# Partially_ordered_set

In mathematics, especially order theory, a **partially ordered set** (or **poset**) formalizes and generalizes the intuitive concept of an ordering, sequencing, or arrangement of the elements of a set. A poset consists of a set together with a binary relation that indicates that, for certain pairs of elements in the set, one of the elements precedes the other. Such a relation is called a *partial order* to reflect the fact that not every pair of elements need be related: for some pairs, it may be that neither element precedes the other in the poset. Thus, partial orders generalize the more familiar total orders, in which every pair is related. A finite poset can be visualized through its Hasse diagram, which depicts the ordering relation.

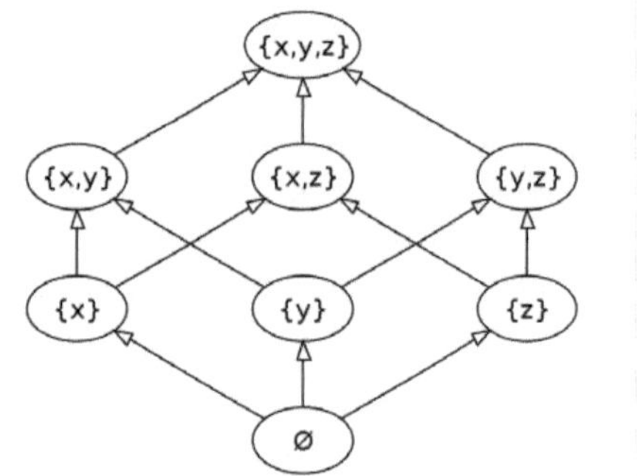

The Hasse diagram of the set of all subsets of a three-element set {x, y, z}, ordered by inclusion.

A familiar real-life example of a partially ordered set is a collection of people ordered by genealogical descendancy. Some pairs of people bear the descendant-ancestor relationship, but other pairs bear no such relationship.

## Formal definition

A **partial order** is a binary relation "≤" over a set $P$ which is reflexive, antisymmetric, and transitive, i.e., for all $a$, $b$, and $c$ in $P$, we have that:

- $a \leq a$ (reflexivity);
- if $a \leq b$ and $b \leq a$ then $a = b$ (antisymmetry);
- if $a \leq b$ and $b \leq c$ then $a \leq c$ (transitivity).

In other words, a partial order is an antisymmetric preorder.

A set with a partial order is called a **partially ordered set** (also called a **poset**). The term *ordered set* is sometimes also used for posets, as long as it is clear from the context that no other kinds of orders are meant. In particular, totally ordered sets can also be referred to as "ordered sets", especially in areas where these structures are more common than posets.

For $a$, $b$, elements of a partially ordered set $P$, if $a \leq b$ or $b \leq a$, then $a$ and $b$ are **comparable**. Otherwise they are **incomparable**. A partial order under which every pair of elements is comparable is called a Total order or **linear order**; a totally ordered set is also called a **chain** (e.g., the natural numbers with their standard order). A poset in which no two distinct elements are comparable is called an antichain.

# Examples

Standard examples of posets arising in mathematics include:

- The real numbers ordered by the standard *less-than-or-equal* relation $\leq$ (a totally ordered set as well).
- The set of natural numbers equipped with the relation of divisibility.
- The vertex set of a directed acyclic graph ordered by reachability.
- The set of subsets of a given set (its power set) ordered by inclusion (see the figure on top-right).
- The set of subspaces of a vector space ordered by inclusion.
- For a partially ordered set $P$, the sequence space containing all sequences of elements from $P$, where sequence $a$ precedes sequence $b$ if every item in $a$ precedes the corresponding item in $b$. Formally, $\left(a_n\right)_{n\in} \leq \left(b_n\right)_{n\in}$ if and only if $a_n \leq b_n$ for all $n$ in .
- For a set $X$ and a partially ordered set $P$, the function space containing all functions from $X$ to $P$, where $f \leq g$ if and only if $f(x) \leq g(x)$ for all $x$ in $X$.
- A fence, a partially ordered set defined by an alternating sequence of order relations $a < b > c < d$ ...

# Extrema

There are several notions of "greatest" and "least" element in a poset $P$, notably:

- Greatest element and least element: An element $g$ in $P$ is a greatest element if for every element $a$ in $P$, $a \leq g$. An element $m$ in $P$ is a least element if for every element $a$ in $P$, $a \geq m$. A poset can only have one greatest or least element.
- Maximal elements and minimal elements: An element $g$ in P is a maximal element if there is no element $a$ in $P$ such that $a > g$. Similarly, an element $m$ in $P$ is a minimal element if there is no element $a$ in P such that $a < m$. If a poset has a greatest element, it must be the unique maximal element, but otherwise there can be more than one maximal element, and similarly for least elements and minimal elements.
- Upper and lower bounds: For a subset $A$ of $P$, an element $x$ in $P$ is an upper bound of $A$ if $a \leq x$, for each element $a$ in $A$. In particular, $x$ need not be in $A$ to be an upper bound of $A$. Similarly, an element $x$ in $P$ is a lower bound of $A$ if $a \geq x$, for each element $a$ in $A$. A greatest element of $P$ is an upper bound of $P$ itself, and a least element is a lower bound of $P$.

For example, consider the positive integers, ordered by divisibility: 1 is a least element, as it divides all other elements; on the other hand this poset does not have a greatest element (although if one would include 0 in the poset, which is a multiple of any integer, that would be a greatest element). This partially ordered set does not even have any maximal elements, since any $g$ divides for instance $2g$, which is distinct from it, so $g$ is not be maximal. If we exclude the number 1, while keeping divisibility as ordering on the elements greater than 1, then the resulting poset does not have a least element, but any prime number is a minimal element for it. In this poset, 60 is an upper bound (though not a least upper bound) of the subset $\{2,3,5,10\}$, which subset does not have any lower bound (since 1 is not in the poset); on the other hand 2 is a lower bound of the subset of powers of 2, which subset does not have any upper bound.

## Orders on the Cartesian product of partially ordered sets

In order of increasing strength, i.e., decreasing sets of pairs, three of the possible partial orders on the Cartesian product of two partially ordered sets are:

- Lexicographical order: $(a,b) \leq (c,d)$ if and only if $a < c$ or ($a = c$ and $b \leq d$).
- $(a,b) \leq (c,d)$ if and only if $a \leq c$ and $b \leq d$ (the product order).
- $(a,b) \leq (c,d)$ if and only if ($a < c$ and $b < d$) or ($a = c$ and $b = d$) (the reflexive closure of the direct product of the corresponding strict orders).

All three can similarly be defined for the Cartesian product of more than two sets.

Applied to ordered vector spaces over the same field, the result is in each case also an ordered vector space.

See also orders on the Cartesian product of totally ordered sets.

## Strict and non-strict partial orders

In some contexts, the partial order defined above is called a **non-strict** (or **reflexive**, or **weak**) **partial order**. In these contexts a **strict** (or **irreflexive**) **partial order** "<" is a binary relation that is irreflexive and transitive, and therefore asymmetric. In other words, asymmetric (hence irreflexive) and transitive.

Thus, for all $a$, $b$, and $c$ in $P$, we have that:

- $\neg(a < a)$ (irreflexivity);
- if $a < b$ then $\neg(b < a)$ (asymmetry); and
- if $a < b$ and $b < c$ then $a < c$ (transitivity).

There is a 1-to-1 correspondence between all non-strict and strict partial orders.

If "$\leq$" is a non-strict partial order, then the corresponding strict partial order "<" is the reflexive reduction given by:

$$a < b \text{ if and only if } (a \leq b \text{ and } a \neq b)$$

Conversely, if "<" is a strict partial order, then the corresponding non-strict partial order "$\leq$" is the reflexive closure given by:

$$a \leq b \text{ if and only if } a < b \text{ or } a = b.$$

This is the reason for using the notation "$\leq$".

Strict partial orders are useful because they correspond more directly to directed acyclic graphs (dags): every strict partial order is a dag, and the transitive closure of a dag is both a strict partial order and also a dag itself.

## Inverse and order dual

The inverse or converse $\geq$ of a partial order relation $\leq$ satisfies $x \geq y$ if and only if $y \leq x$. The inverse of a partial order relation is reflexive, transitive, and antisymmetric, and hence itself a partial order relation. The *order dual* of a partially ordered set is the same set with the partial order relation replaced by its inverse. The irreflexive relation > is to $\geq$ as < is to $\leq$.

Any one of these four relations $\leq$, <, $\geq$, and > on a given set uniquely determine the other three.

In general two elements $x$ and $y$ of a partial order may stand in any of four mutually exclusive relationships to each other: either $x < y$, or $x = y$, or $x > y$, or $x$ and $y$ are *incomparable* (none of the other three). A totally ordered set is one that rules out this fourth possibility: all pairs of elements are comparable and we then say that trichotomy holds. The natural numbers, the integers, the rationals, and the reals are all totally ordered by their algebraic (signed) magnitude whereas the complex numbers are not. This is not to say that the complex numbers cannot be totally ordered; we could for example order them lexicographically via $x+iy < u+iv$ if and only if $x < u$ or ($x = u$ and $y < v$), but this is not ordering by magnitude in any reasonable sense as it makes 1 greater than 100i. Ordering them by absolute magnitude yields a preorder in which all pairs are comparable, but this is not a partial order since 1 and i have the same absolute magnitude but are not equal, violating antisymmetry.

## Number of partial orders

Sequence A001035 [1] in OEIS gives the number of partial orders on a set of $n$ labeled elements:

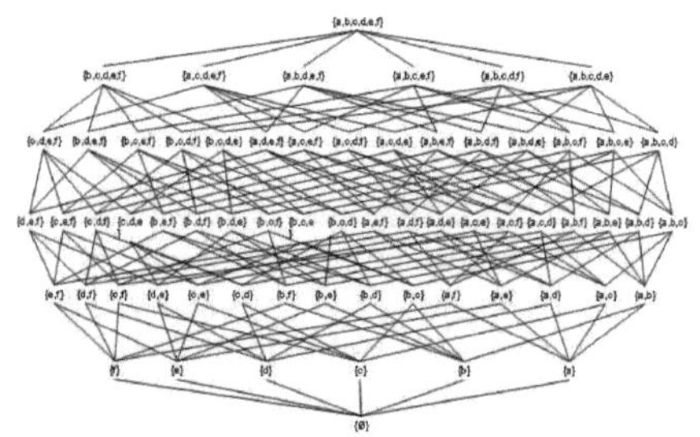

Partially ordered set of set of all subsets of a six-element set {a, b, c, d, e, f}, ordered by the subset relation.

| Number of $n$-element binary relations of different types | | | | | | | |
|---|---|---|---|---|---|---|---|
| $n$ | all | transitive | reflexive | preorder | partial order | total preorder | total order | equivalence relation |
| 0 | 1 | 1 | 1 | 1 | 1 | 1 | 1 | 1 |
| 1 | 2 | 2 | 1 | 1 | 1 | 1 | 1 | 1 |
| 2 | 16 | 13 | 4 | 4 | 3 | 3 | 2 | 2 |
| 3 | 512 | 171 | 64 | 29 | 19 | 13 | 6 | 5 |
| 4 | 65536 | 3994 | 4096 | 355 | 219 | 75 | 24 | 15 |
| OEIS | A002416 | A006905 | A053763 | A000798 | A001035 | A000670 | A000142 | A000110 |

The number of strict partial orders is the same as that of partial orders.

If we count only up to isomorphism, we get 1, 1, 2, 5, 16, 63, 318, ... (sequence A000112 in OEIS).

## Linear extension

A partial order $\le^*$ on a set $X$ is an **extension** of another partial order $\le$ on $X$ provided that for all elements $x$ and $y$ of $X$, whenever $x \le y$, it is also the case that $x \le^* y$. A linear extension is an extension that is also a linear (i.e., total) order. Every partial order can be extended to a total order (order-extension principle).[2]

In computer science, algorithms for finding linear extensions of partial orders (represented as the reachability orders of directed acyclic graphs) are called topological sorting.

## In category theory

Every poset (and every preorder) may be considered as a category in which every hom-set has at most one element. More explicitly, let hom($x$, $y$) = {($x$, $y$)} if $x \le y$ (and otherwise the empty set) and ($y$, $z$)o($x$, $y$) = ($x$, $z$). Posets are equivalent to one another if and only if they are isomorphic. In a poset, the smallest element, if it exists, is an initial object, and the largest element, if it exists, is a terminal object. Also, every preordered set is equivalent to a poset. Finally, every subcategory of a poset is isomorphism-closed.

A functor from a poset category (a diagram indexed by a poset category) is a commutative diagram.

## Partial orders in topological spaces

If $P$ is a partially ordered set that has also been given the structure of a topological space, then it is customary to assume that $\{(a, b)\ a \le b\}$ is a closed subset of the topological product space . Under this assumption partial order relations are well behaved at limits in the sense that if , and $a_i \le b_i$ for all $i$, then $a \le b$.[3]

## Interval

For $a \le b$, the closed interval $[a,b]$ is the set of elements $x$ satisfying $a \le x \le b$ (i.e. $a \le x$ and $x \le b$). It contains at least the elements $a$ and $b$.

Using the corresponding strict relation "<", the open interval $(a,b)$ is the set of elements $x$ satisfying $a < x < b$ (i.e. $a < x$ and $x < b$). An open interval may be empty even if $a < b$. For example, the open interval $(1,2)$ on the integers is empty since there are no integers $i$ such that $1 < i < 2$.

Sometimes the definitions are extended to allow $a > b$, in which case the interval is empty.

The *half-open intervals* $[a,b)$ and $(a,b]$ are defined similarly.

A poset is locally finite if every interval is finite. For example, the integers are locally finite under their natural ordering.

This concept of an interval in a partial order should not be confused with the particular class of partial orders known as the interval orders.

## See also

- antimatroid, a formalization of orderings on a set that allows more general families of orderings than posets
- causal set
- comparability graph
- directed set
- graded poset
- semilattice
- lattice
- ordered group
- poset topology, a kind of topological space that can be defined from any poset
- semiorder
- series-parallel partial order
- strict weak ordering - strict partial order "<" in which the relation "neither $a < b$ nor $b < a$" is transitive.
- complete partial order

## Notes

[1] http://en.wikipedia.org/wiki/Oeis%3Aa001035
[2] Jech, Thomas (2008) [originally published in 1973]. *The Axiom of Choice*. Dover Publications. ISBN 0-486-46624-8.
[3] Ward, L. E. Jr (1954). "Partially Ordered Topological Spaces". *Proceedings of the American Mathematical Society* **5** (1): 144–161. doi:10.1090/S0002-9939-1954-0063016-5

## References

- Deshpande, Jayant V. (1968). "On Continuity of a Partial Order". *Proceedings of the American Mathematical Society* **19** (2): 383–386. doi:10.1090/S0002-9939-1968-0236071-7.
- Schröder, Bernd S. W. (2003). *Ordered Sets: An Introduction*. Birkhäuser, Boston.

- Stanley, Richard P.. *Enumerative Combinatorics 1*. Cambridge Studies in Advanced Mathematics. **49**. Cambridge University Press. ISBN 0-521-66351-2.

## External links

- Sequences in the OEIS:

  A001035: Number of posets with *n* labeled elements

  A000112: Number of posets with *n* unlabeled elements

# Indeterminacy_in_concurrent_computation

**Indeterminacy in concurrent computation** is concerned with the effects of indeterminacy in concurrent computation.

Computation is an area in which indeterminacy is becoming increasingly important because of the massive increase in concurrency due to networking and the advent of many-core computer architectures. These computer systems make use of arbiters which give rise to indeterminacy.

## A limitation of logic programming

Patrick Hayes [1973] argued that the "usual sharp distinction that is made between the processes of computation and deduction, is misleading". Robert Kowalski developed the thesis that *computation could be subsumed by deduction* and quoted with approval "Computation is controlled deduction." which he attributed to Hayes in his 1988 paper on the early history of Prolog. Contrary to Kowalski and Hayes, Carl Hewitt claimed that logical deduction was incapable of carrying out concurrent computation in open systems.

Hewitt [1985], Hewitt and Agha [1991], and other published work argued that mathematical models of concurrency did not determine particular concurrent computations as follows: The Actor model makes use of arbitration (often in the form of notional Arbiters) for determining which message is next in the arrival ordering of an Actor that is sent multiple messages concurrently. This introduces indeterminacy in the arrival order. Since the arrival orderings are indeterminate, they cannot be deduced from prior information by mathematical logic alone. Therefore mathematical logic can not implement concurrent computation in open systems.

The authors note that although mathematical logic cannot, in their view, implement general concurrency it can implement some special cases of concurrent computation, *e.g.,* sequential computation and some kinds of parallel computation including the lambda calculus.

## Arrival order indeterminacy

According to Hewitt [2008], in concrete terms for Actor systems, typically we cannot observe the details by which the arrival order of messages for an Actor is determined. Attempting to do so affects the results and can even push the indeterminacy elsewhere. e.g., see metastability in electronics and arbiters. Instead of observing the internals of arbitration processes of Actor computations, we await outcomes. Indeterminacy in arbiters produces indeterminacy in Actors. The reason that we await outcomes is that we have no alternative because of indeterminacy.

It is important to be clear about the basis for the published claim about the limitation of mathematical logic. It was not just that Actors could not in general be implemented in mathematical logic. The published claim was that because of the indeterminacy of the physical basis of the Actor model, that no kind of deductive mathematical logic could escape the limitation. This became important later when researchers attempted to extend Prolog (which had some basis in logic programming) to concurrent computation using message passing. (See the section below).

What does the mathematical theory of Actors have to say about this? A *closed* system is defined to be one which does not communicate with the outside. Actor model theory provides the means to characterize all the possible computations of a closed Actor system using the Representation Theorem [Hewitt 2007] as follows:

> The mathematical denotation denoted by a closed system $S$ is found by constructing increasingly better approximations from an initial behavior called $\perp_S$ using a behavior approximating function **progression**$_S$ to construct a denotation (meaning ) for $S$ as follows :

$$\mathbf{Denote}_S \equiv \sqcup_{i \in \omega} \mathbf{progression}_S^{\ i} (\perp_S)$$

In this way, the behavior of $S$ can be mathematically characterized in terms of all its possible behaviors (including those involving unbounded nondeterminism).

So mathematical logic can characterize (as opposed to implement) all the possible computations of a closed Actor system.

## A limitation of logic due to lack of information

An open Actor system $S$ is one in which the addresses of outside Actors can be passed into $S$ in the middle of computations so that $S$ can communicate with these outside Actors. These outside Actors can then in turn communicate with Actors internal to $S$ using addresses supplied to them by $S$. Due to limitation of the inability to deduce arrival orderings, knowledge of what messages are sent from outside would not enable the response of $S$ to be deduced. When other models of concurrent systems ( *e.g.,* process calculi) are used to implement open systems, these systems also can have behavior that depends on arrival time orderings and so cannot be implemented by logical deduction.

## Prolog-like concurrent systems were claimed to be based on mathematical logic

Keith Clark, Hervé Gallaire, Steve Gregory, Vijay Saraswat, Udi Shapiro, Kazunori Ueda, etc. developed a family of Prolog-like concurrent message passing systems using unification of shared variables and data structure streams for messages. Claims were made that these systems were based on mathematical logic. This kind of system was used as the basis of the Japanese Fifth Generation Project (ICOT).

Carl Hewitt and Gul Agha [1991] argued that these Prolog-like concurrent systems were neither deductive nor logical: like the Actor model, the Prolog-like concurrent systems were based on message passing and consequently were subject to the same indeterminacy.

## Logical operations and system efficiency

Hewitt maintained that a basic lesson can be learned from Prolog and the Prolog-like concurrent systems: a universal model of concurrent computation is limited by having any mandatory overhead in the basic communication mechanisms. This is an argument against including pattern-directed invocation using unification and extraction of messages from data structure streams as fundamental primitives. But compare Shapiro's survey of Prolog-like concurrent programming languages for arguments for inclusion.

# Indeterminacy in other models of computation

Arbitration is the basis of the indeterminacy in the Actor model of concurrent computation (see Actor model early history and Actor model theory). It may also play a role in other models of concurrent systems such as process calculi.

# See also

- Quantum computer
- Randomized algorithm
- Nondeterministic Turing machine

# References


- Carl Hewitt. **PLANNER: A Language for Proving Theorems in Robots** IJCAI 1969.
- Carl Hewitt. **Procedural Embedding of Knowledge In Planner** IJCAI 1971.
- Carl Hewitt, Peter Bishop and Richard Steiger. **A Universal Modular Actor Formalism for Artificial Intelligence** IJCAI 1973.
- Robert Kowalski **Predicate Logic as Programming Language** Memo 70, Department of Artificial Intelligence, Edinburgh University. 1973.
- Pat Hayes. **Computation and Deduction** Mathematical Foundations of Computer Science: Proceedings of Symposium and Summer School, Štrbské Pleso, High Tatras, Czechoslovakia, September 3-8, 1973.
- Carl Hewitt and Henry Baker **Laws for Communicating Parallel Processes** IFIP-77, August 1977.
- Carl Hewitt. **Viewing Control Structures as Patterns of Passing Messages** Journal of Artificial Intelligence. June 1977.
- Henry Baker. **Actor Systems for Real-Time Computation** MIT EECS Doctoral Dissertation. January 1978.
- Bill Kornfeld and Carl Hewitt. **The Scientific Community Metaphor** IEEE Transactions on Systems, Man, and Cybernetics. January 1981.
- Will Clinger. **Foundations of Actor Semantics** MIT Mathematics Doctoral Dissertation. June 1981.
- Carl Hewitt. **The Challenge of Open Systems** Byte Magazine. April 1985. Reprinted in *The foundation of artificial intelligence---a sourcebook* Cambridge University Press. 1990.
- Gul Agha. **Actors: A Model of Concurrent Computation in Distributed Systems** [1] Doctoral Dissertation. MIT Press. 1986.
- Robert Kowalski. **The limitation of logic** Proceedings of the 1986 ACM 14th Annual Conference on Computer science.
- Ehud Shapiro (Editor). **Concurrent Prolog** MIT Press. 1987.
- Robert Kowalski. **The Early Years of Logic Programming** Communications of the ACM. January 1988.
- Ehud Shapiro. **The family of concurrent logic programming languages** ACM Computing Surveys. September 1989.
- Carl Hewitt and Gul Agha. **Guarded Horn clause languages: are they deductive and Logical?** International Conference on Fifth Generation Computer Systems, Ohmsha 1988. Tokyo. Also in *Artificial Intelligence at MIT*, Vol. 2. MIT Press 1991.
- Carl Hewitt. *Carl Hewitt. **The repeated demise of logic programming and why it will be reincarnated** What Went Wrong and Why: Lessons from AI Research and Applications. Technical Report SS-06-08. AAAI Press. March 2006.

## References

[1]  https://dspace.mit.edu/handle/1721.1/6952

# Lambda_calculus

The **lambda calculus** (also written as **λ-calculus**) is a formal system in mathematical logic for expressing computation by way of variable binding and substitution. It was first formulated by Alonzo Church as a way to formalize mathematics through the notion of functions, in contrast to the field of set theory. Although not very successful in that respect, the lambda calculus found early successes in the area of computability theory, such as a negative answer to Hilbert's Entscheidungsproblem.

Because of the importance of the notion of variable binding and substitution, there is not just one system of lambda calculus. Historically, the most important system was the untyped lambda calculus. In the untyped lambda calculus, function application has no restrictions (so the notion of the domain of a function is not built into the system). In the Church–Turing Thesis, the untyped lambda calculus is claimed to be capable of computing all effectively calculable functions. The typed lambda calculus is a variety that restricts function application, so that functions can only be applied if they are capable of accepting the given input's "type" of data.

Today, the lambda calculus has applications in many different areas in mathematics, philosophy, and computer science. It is still used in the area of computability theory, although Turing machines are arguably the preferred model for computation. Lambda calculus has played an important role in the development of the theory of programming languages. The most prominent counterparts to lambda calculus in computer science are functional programming languages, which essentially implement the calculus (augmented with some constants and datatypes). Beyond programming languages, the lambda calculus also has many applications in proof theory. A major example of this is the Curry–Howard correspondence, which gives a correspondence between different systems of typed lambda calculi and systems of formal logic.

## Lambda calculus in history of mathematics

The lambda calculus was introduced by mathematician Alonzo Church in the 1930s as part of an investigation into the foundations of mathematics.[1] [2] The original system was shown to be logically inconsistent in 1935 when Stephen Kleene and J. B. Rosser developed the Kleene–Rosser paradox.

Subsequently, in 1936 Church isolated and published just the portion relevant to computation, what is now called the untyped lambda calculus.[3] In 1940, he also introduced a computationally weaker, but logically consistent system, known as the simply typed lambda calculus.[4]

## Informal description

### Motivation

Recursive functions are a fundamental concept within computer science and mathematics. The λ-calculus provides simple semantics for computation, enabling properties of computation to be studied formally.

Consider the following two examples. The identity function

takes a single input, , and immediately returns (i.e. the identity does nothing with its input), whereas the function

takes a pair of inputs, and and returns the sum of their squares, . Using these two examples, we can make some useful observations that motivate the major ideas in the lambda calculus.

The first observation is that functions need not be explicitly named. That is, the function

can be rewritten in *anonymous form* as

(read as "the pair of and is mapped to "). Similarly,

can be rewritten in anonymous form as , where the input is simply mapped to itself.

The second observation is that the specific choice of name for a function's arguments is largely irrelevant. That is,

and

express the same function: the identity. Similarly,

and

also express the same function.

Finally, any function that requires two inputs, for instance the before mentioned function, can be reworked into an equivalent function that accepts a single input, and as output returns *another* function, that in turn accepts a single input. For example,

can be reworked into

This transformation is called currying, i.e. transforming a function that takes multiple arguments in such a way that it can be called as a *chain of* functions *each with a single argument* (partial application). It can be generalized to functions accepting an arbitrary number of arguments.

Currying may be best grasped intuitively through the use of an example. Compare the function

with its curried form,

Applying the function to the arguments (5, 2), we have:

However, using currying, we have:

and we see the uncurried and curried forms compute the same result. Notice that x*x became a constant after the first argument assignment.

## The lambda calculus

The lambda calculus consists of a language of **lambda terms** along with an equational theory (which can also be understood operationally).

Since the names of functions are largely a convenience, the lambda calculus has no means of naming a function. Since all functions expecting more than one input can be transformed into equivalent functions accepting a single input (via Currying), the lambda calculus has no means for creating a function that accepts more than one argument. Since the names of arguments are largely irrelevant, the native notion of equality on lambda terms is **alpha-equivalence** (see below), which codifies this principle.

### Lambda terms

The syntax of lambda terms is particularly simple. There are three ways in which to obtain them:

- a lambda term may be a variable, $x$;
- if $t$ is a lambda term, and $x$ is a variable, then $\lambda x . t$ is a lambda term (called a **lambda abstraction**);
- if $t$ and $s$ are lambda terms, then $t s$ is a lambda term (called an **application**).

Nothing else is a lambda term, though bracketing may be used and may be needed to disambiguate terms. For example, $\lambda x . (x (\lambda x . x))$ and $(\lambda x . x)(\lambda x . x)$ denote different terms.

Intuitively, a lambda abstraction $\lambda x . t$ represents an anonymous function that takes a single input, and the $\lambda$ is said to **bind** $x$ in $t$, and an application $t s$ represents the application of input $s$ to some function $t$. In the lambda calculus, functions are taken to be **first class values**, so functions may be used as the inputs to other functions, and functions may return functions as their outputs.

For example, $\lambda x . x$ represents the identity function, $x \mapsto x$, and $(\lambda x . x) y$ represents the identity function applied to $y$. Further, $(\lambda x . y)$ represents the **constant function** $x \mapsto y$, the function that always returns y, no matter the input. It should be noted that function application is left-associative, so $(\lambda x.x)\, y\, z\; =\; ((\lambda x.x)\, y)\, z.$

Lambda terms on their own aren't particularly interesting. What makes them interesting are the various notions of **equivalence** and **reduction** that can be defined over them.

### Alpha equivalence

A basic form of equivalence, definable on lambda terms, is alpha equivalence. It captures the intuition that the particular choice of a bound variable, in a lambda abstraction, doesn't (usually) matter. For instance, $\lambda x.x$ and $\lambda y.y$ are alpha-equivalent lambda terms, representing the same identity function. Note that the terms $x$ and $y$ **aren't** alpha-equivalent, because they are not bound in a lambda abstraction. In many presentations, it is usual to identify alpha-equivalent lambda terms.

The following definitions are necessary in order to be able to define beta reduction.

### Free variables

The **free variables** of a term are those variables not bound by a lambda abstraction. That is, the free variables of $x$ are just $x$; the free variables of $\lambda x.t$ are the free variables of $t$, with $x$ removed, and the free variables of $ts$ are the union of the free variables of $t$ and $s$.

For example, the lambda term representing the identity $\lambda x.x$ has no free variables, but the constant function $\lambda x.y$ has a single free variable, $y$.

### Capture-avoiding substitutions

Using the definition of free variables, we may now define a capture-avoiding substitution. Suppose $t$, $s$ and $r$ are lambda terms and $x$ and $y$ are variables. We write $t[x := r]$ for the substitution of $r$ for $x$ in $t$, in a capture-avoiding manner. That is:

- $x[x := r] = r$;
- $y[x := r] = y$ if $x \neq y$;
- $(ts)[x := r] = (t[x := r])(s[x := r])$;
- $(\lambda x.t)[x := r] = \lambda x.t$;
- $(\lambda y.t)[x := r] = \lambda y.(t[x := r])$ if $x \neq y$ and $y$ is not in the free variables of $r$ (sometimes said "$y$ is fresh for $r$").

For example, $(\lambda x.x)[y := y] = \lambda x.(x[y := y]) = \lambda x.x$, and $((\lambda x.y)x)[x := y] = ((\lambda x.y)[x := y])(x[x := y]) = (\lambda x.y)y.$

The freshness condition (requiring that $y$ is not in the free variables of $r$) is crucial in order to ensure that substitution does not change the meaning of functions. For example, suppose we define another substitution action without the freshness condition. Then, $(\lambda x.y)[y := x] = \lambda x.(y[y := x]) = \lambda x.x$, and the constant function $\lambda x.y$ turns into the identity $\lambda x.x$ by substitution.

If our freshness condition is not met, then we may simply alpha-rename with a suitably fresh variable. For example, switching back to our correct notion of substitution, in $(\lambda x.y)[y := x]$ the lambda abstraction can be renamed with a fresh variable $z$, to obtain $(\lambda z.y)[y := x] = \lambda z.(y[y := x]) = \lambda z.x$, and the meaning of the function is preserved by substitution.

**Beta reduction**

Beta reduction states that an application of the form $(\lambda x.t)\,s$ reduces to the term $t[x := s]$ (we write $(\lambda x.t)\,s \rightarrow t[x := s]$ as a convenient shorthand for "$(\lambda x.t)\,s$ beta reduces to $t[x := s]$"). For example, for every $s$ we have $(\lambda x.x)\,s \rightarrow x[x := s] = s$, demonstrating that $\lambda x.x$ really is the identity. Similarly, $(\lambda x.y)\,s \rightarrow y[x := s] = y$, demonstrating that $\lambda x.y$ really is a constant function.

The lambda calculus may be seen as an idealised functional programming language, like Haskell or Standard ML. Under this view, beta reduction corresponds to a computational step, and in the untyped lambda calculus, as presented here, reduction need not terminate. For instance, consider the term $(\lambda x.xx)\,(\lambda x.xx)$. Here, we have $(\lambda x.xx)\,(\lambda x.xx) \rightarrow (xx)[x := \lambda x.xx] = (x[x := \lambda x.xx])(x[x := \lambda x.xx]) = (\lambda x.xx)\,(\lambda x.xx)$. That is, the term reduces to itself in a single beta reduction, and therefore reduction will never terminate.

Another problem with the untyped lambda calculus is the inability to distinguish between different kinds of data. For instance, we may want to write a function that only operates on numbers. However, in the untyped lambda calculus, there's no way to prevent our function from being applied to truth values, or strings, for instance.

Typed lambda calculi, which will be introduced later in the article, have the property that if a term is well-typed, then it never gets "stuck" (where there is no evaluation rule for the term), and that if a term $e$ has a particular type, and $e \rightarrow e$, then $e$ has the same type.

# Formal definition

## Definition

Lambda expressions are composed of

> variables $v_1$, $v_2$, ..., $v_n$, ...
>
> the abstraction symbols $\lambda$ and .
>
> parentheses ( )

The set of lambda expressions, $\Lambda$, can be defined recursively:

1. If x is a variable, then $x \in \Lambda$
2. If x is a variable and $M \in \Lambda$, then $(\lambda x.M) \in \Lambda$
3. If M, N $\in \Lambda$, then (M N) $\in \Lambda$

Instances of rule 2 are known as abstractions and instances of rule 3 are known as applications.[5]

## Notation

To keep the notation of lambda expressions uncluttered, the following conventions are usually applied.

* Outermost parentheses are dropped: M N instead of (M N).
* Applications are assumed to be left associative: M N P may be written instead of ((M N) P).[6]
* The body of an abstraction extends as far right as possible: λx.M N means λx.(M N) and not (λx.M) N.
* A sequence of abstractions is contracted: λx.λy.λz.N is abbreviated as λxyz.N.[7] [8]

### Free and bound variables

The abstraction operator, λ, is said to bind its variable wherever it occurs in the body of the abstraction. Variables that fall within the scope of a lambda are said to be *bound*. All other variables are called *free*. For example in the following expression y is a bound variable and x is free: $\lambda y.\, x\, x\, y$. Also note that a variable binds to its "nearest" lambda. In the following expression one single occurrence of x is bound by the second lambda: $\lambda x.\, y\ (\lambda x.\, z\, x)$

The set of *free variables* of a lambda expression, M, is denoted as FV(M) and is defined by recursion on the structure of the terms, as follows:

1. FV(x) = {x}, where x is a variable
2. FV(λx.M) = FV(M) \ {x}
3. FV(M N) = FV(M) ∪ FV(N)[9]

An expression that contains no free variables is said to be *closed*. Closed lambda expressions are also known as combinators and are equivalent to terms in combinatory logic.

# Reduction

The meaning of lambda expressions is defined by how expressions can be reduced.[10]

There are three kinds of reduction:

- **α-conversion**: changing bound variables;
- **β-reduction**: applying functions to their arguments;
- **η-conversion**: which captures a notion of extensionality.

We also speak of the resulting equivalences: two expressions are *β-equivalent*, if they can be β-converted into the same expression, and α/η-equivalence are defined similarly.

The term *redex*, short for *reducible expression*, refers to subterms that can be reduced by one of the reduction rules. For example, $(\lambda x.M)$ N is a beta-redex; if $x$ is not free in M, $\lambda x.M\ x$ is an eta-redex. The expression to which a redex reduces is called its reduct; using the previous example, the reducts of these expressions are respectively `M[x:=N]` and M.

### α-conversion

Alpha-conversion, sometimes known as alpha-renaming,[11] allows bound variable names to be changed. For example, alpha-conversion of $\lambda x.x$ might yield $\lambda y.y$. Terms that differ only by alpha-conversion are called *α-equivalent*. Frequently in uses of lambda calculus, α-equivalent terms are considered to be equivalent.

The precise rules for alpha-conversion are not completely trivial. First, when alpha-converting an abstraction, the only variable occurrences that are renamed are those that are bound to the same abstraction. For example, an alpha-conversion of $\lambda x.\lambda x.x$ could result in $\lambda y.\lambda x.x$, but it could *not* result in $\lambda y.\lambda x.y$. The latter has a different meaning from the original.

Second, alpha-conversion is not possible if it would result in a variable getting captured by a different abstraction. For example, if we replace $x$ with $y$ in $\lambda x.\lambda y.x$, we get $\lambda y.\lambda y.y$, which is not at all the same.

In programming languages with static scope, alpha-conversion can be used to make name resolution simpler by ensuring that no variable name masks a name in a containing scope (see alpha renaming to make name resolution trivial).

### Substitution

Substitution, written $E[V := E']$, is the process of replacing all free occurrences of the variable $V$ by expression $E'$. Substitution on terms of the $\lambda$-calculus is defined by recursion on the structure of terms, as follows.

```
x[x := N]            ≡ N
y[x := N]            ≡ y, if x ≠ y
(M₁ M₂)[x := N]     ≡ (M₁[x := N]) (M₂[x := N])
(λx.M)[x := N]       ≡ λx.(M)
(λy.M)[x := N]       ≡ λy.(M[x := N]), if x ≠ y, provided y ∉ FV(N)
```

To substitute into a lambda abstraction, it is sometimes necessary to $\alpha$-convert the expression. For example, it is not correct for $(\lambda x. y)[y := x]$ to result in $(\lambda x. x)$, because the substituted $x$ was supposed to be free but ended up being bound. The correct substitution in this case is $(\lambda z. x)$, up to $\alpha$-equivalence. Notice that substitution is defined uniquely up to $\alpha$-equivalence.

## β-reduction

Beta-reduction captures the idea of function application. Beta-reduction is defined in terms of substitution: the beta-reduction of $((\lambda V. E)\ E')$ is $E[V := E']$.

For example, assuming some encoding of $2$, $7$, $\times$, we have the following $\beta$-reductions: $((\lambda n. n \times 2)\ 7) \rightarrow 7 \times 2$.

## η-conversion

Eta-conversion expresses the idea of extensionality, which in this context is that two functions are the same if and only if they give the same result for all arguments. Eta-conversion converts between $\lambda x. (f\ x)$ and $f$ whenever $x$ does not appear free in $f$.

# Normal forms and confluence

For the untyped lambda calculus, $\beta$-reduction as a rewriting rule is neither strongly normalising nor weakly normalising.

However, it can be shown that $\beta$-reduction is confluent. (Of course, we are working up to $\alpha$-conversion, i.e. we consider two normal forms to be equal, if it is possible to $\alpha$-convert one into the other.)

Therefore, both strongly normalising terms and weakly normalising terms have a unique normal form. For strongly normalising terms, any reduction strategy is guaranteed to yield the normal form, whereas for weakly normalising terms, some reduction strategies may fail to find it.

# Encoding datatypes

The basic lambda calculus may be used to model booleans, arithmetic, data structures and recursion, as illustrated in the following sub-sections.

## Arithmetic in lambda calculus

There are several possible ways to define the natural numbers in lambda calculus, but by far the most common are the Church numerals, which can be defined as follows:

```
0 := λf.λx.x
1 := λf.λx.f x
2 := λf.λx.f (f x)
```

```
3 := λf.λx.f (f (f x))
```

and so on. Or using the alternate syntax presented above in Notation:

```
0 := λfx.x

1 := λfx.f x

2 := λfx.f (f x)

3 := λfx.f (f (f x))
```

A Church numeral is a higher-order function—it takes a single-argument function $f$, and returns another single-argument function. The Church numeral $n$ is a function that takes a function $f$ as argument and returns the $n$-th composition of $f$, i.e. the function $f$ composed with itself $n$ times. This is denoted $f^{(n)}$ and is in fact the $n$-th power of $f$ (considered as an operator); $f^{(0)}$ is defined to be the identity function. Such repeated compositions (of a single function $f$) obey the laws of exponents, which is why these numerals can be used for arithmetic. (In Church's original lambda calculus, the formal parameter of a lambda expression was required to occur at least once in the function body, which made the above definition of $0$ impossible.)

We can define a successor function, which takes a number $n$ and returns $n + 1$ by adding an additional application of $f$:

```
SUCC := λn.λf.λx.f (n f x)
```

Because the $m$-th composition of $f$ composed with the $n$-th composition of $f$ gives the $m+n$-th composition of $f$, addition can be defined as follows:

```
PLUS := λm.λn.λf.λx.m f (n f x)
```

PLUS can be thought of as a function taking two natural numbers as arguments and returning a natural number; it can be verified that

```
PLUS 2 3
```

and

```
5
```

are equivalent lambda expressions. Since adding $m$ to a number $n$ can be accomplished by adding 1 $m$ times, an equivalent definition is:

```
PLUS := λm.λn.m SUCC n[12]
```

Similarly, multiplication can be defined as

```
MULT := λm.λn.λf.m (n f) [13]
```

Alternatively

```
MULT := λm.λn.m (PLUS n) 0
```

since multiplying $m$ and $n$ is the same as repeating the add $n$ function $m$ times and then applying it to zero. Exponentiation has a rather simple rendering in Church numerals, namely

```
POW := λb.λe.e b
```

The predecessor function defined by PRED $n = n - 1$ for a positive integer $n$ and PRED $0 = 0$ is considerably more difficult. The formula

```
PRED := λn.λf.λx.n (λg.λh.h (g f)) (λu.x) (λu.u)
```

can be validated by showing inductively that if $T$ denotes $(λg.λh.h (g f))$, then $T^{(n)} (λu.x) = (λh.h(f^{(n-1)} (x)))$ for $n > 0$. Two other definitions of PRED are given below, one using conditionals and the other using pairs. With the predecessor function, subtraction is straightforward. Defining

```
SUB := λm.λn.n PRED m,
```

SUB $m\,n$ yields $m - n$ when $m > n$ and $0$ otherwise.

## Logic and predicates

By convention, the following two definitions (known as Church booleans) are used for the boolean values TRUE and FALSE:

    TRUE  := λx.λy.x

    FALSE := λx.λy.y

> (Note that FALSE is equivalent to the Church numeral zero defined above)

Then, with these two λ-terms, we can define some logic operators (these are just possible formulations; other expressions are equally correct):

    AND := λp.λq.p q p

    OR := λp.λq.p p q

    NOT := λp.λa.λb.p b a

    IFTHENELSE := λp.λa.λb.p a b

We are now able to compute some logic functions, for example:

    AND TRUE FALSE

        ≡ (λp.λq.p q p) TRUE FALSE  →β  TRUE FALSE TRUE

        ≡ (λx.λy.x) FALSE TRUE  →β  FALSE

and we see that AND TRUE FALSE is equivalent to FALSE.

A *predicate* is a function that returns a boolean value. The most fundamental predicate is ISZERO, which returns TRUE if its argument is the Church numeral 0, and FALSE if its argument is any other Church numeral:

    ISZERO := λn.n (λx.FALSE) TRUE

The following predicate tests whether the first argument is less-than-or-equal-to the second:

    LEQ := λm.λn.ISZERO (SUB m n),

and since $m = n$, if LEQ $m$ $n$ and LEQ $n$ $m$, it is straightforward to build a predicate for numerical equality.

The availability of predicates and the above definition of TRUE and FALSE make it convenient to write "if-then-else" expressions in lambda calculus. For example, the predecessor function can be defined as:

    PRED := λn.n (λg.λk.ISZERO (g 1) k (PLUS (g k) 1)) (λv.0) 0

which can be verified by showing inductively that $n$ (λg.λk.ISZERO (g 1) k (PLUS (g k) 1)) (λv.0) is the add $n − 1$ function for $n > 0$.

## Pairs

A pair (2-tuple) can be defined in terms of TRUE and FALSE, by using the Church encoding for pairs. For example, PAIR encapsulates the pair $(x,y)$, FIRST returns the first element of the pair, and SECOND returns the second.

    PAIR := λx.λy.λf.f x y

    FIRST := λp.p TRUE

    SECOND := λp.p FALSE

    NIL := λx.TRUE

    NULL := λp.p (λx.λy.FALSE)

A linked list can be defined as either NIL for the empty list, or the PAIR of an element and a smaller list. The predicate NULL tests for the value NIL. (Alternatively, with NIL := FALSE, the construct $l$ (λh.λt.λz.deal_with_head_h_and_tail_t) (deal_with_nil) obviates the need for an explicit NULL test).

As an example of the use of pairs, the shift-and-increment function that maps $(m,\ n)$ to $(n,\ n + 1)$ can be defined as

```
Φ := λx.PAIR (SECOND x) (SUCC (SECOND x))
```

which allows us to give perhaps the most transparent version of the predecessor function:

```
PRED := λn.FIRST (n Φ (PAIR 0 0)).
```

## Recursion and fixed points

Recursion is the definition of a function using the function itself; on the face of it, lambda calculus does not allow this (we can't refer to a value which is yet to be defined, inside the lambda term defining that same value, as all functions are anonymous in lambda calculus). However, this impression is misleading: in $(λx.x\ x)\ y$ both $x$ 's refer to the same lambda term, $y$, so it is possible for a lambda expression — here $y$ — to be arranged to receive itself as its argument value, through self-application.

Consider for instance the factorial function $F\ (n)$ recursively defined by

```
F(n) = 1, if n = 0; else n × F(n − 1).
```

In lambda expression which is to represent this function, a *parameter* (typically the first one) will be assumed to receive the lambda expression itself as its value, so that calling it — applying it to an argument — will amount to recursion. Thus to achieve recursion, the intended-as-self-referencing argument (called $r$ here) must always be passed to itself within the function body, at a call point:

```
G := λr. λn.(1, if n = 0; else n × (r r (n−1)))
```

$$\text{with } r\ r\ x = F\ x = G\ r\ x \text{ to hold, so } r = G \text{ and}$$

```
F := G G = (λx.x x) G
```

The self-application achieves replication here, passing the function's lambda expression on to the next invocation as an argument value, making it available to be referenced and called there.

This solves the specific problem of the factorial function, but we'd like to have a generic solution, i.e. not forcing a specific re-write for every recursive function:

```
G := λr. λn.(1, if n = 0; else n × (r (n−1)))
```

$$\text{with } r\ x = F\ x = G\ r\ x \text{ to hold, so } r = G\ r =: \text{ FIX G and}$$

```
F := FIX G where FIX g := (r where r = g r) = g (FIX g)
```

$$\text{so that FIX G} = G\ (\text{FIX G}) = (λn.(1, \text{ if } n = 0; \text{ else } n × ((\text{FIX G})(n−1))))$$

Given a lambda term with first argument representing recursive call (e.g. G here), the *fixed-point* combinator `FIX` will return a self-replicating lambda expression representing the recursive function (here, F). The function does not need to be explicitly passed to itself at any point, for the self-replication is arranged in advance, when it is created, to be done each time it is called. Thus the original lambda expression `(FIX G)` is re-created inside itself, at call-point, achieving self-reference.

In fact, there are many possible definitions for this `FIX` operator, the simplest of them being:

```
Y := λg.(λx.g (x x)) (λx.g (x x))
```

In the lambda calculus, $Y\ g$ is a fixed-point of $g$, as it expands to:

```
Y g
λh.((λx.h (x x)) (λx.h (x x))) g
(λx.g (x x)) (λx.g (x x))
g ((λx.g (x x)) (λx.g (x x)))
```

```
g (Y g)
```

Now, to perform our recursive call to the factorial function, we would simply call $(Y\ G)\ n$, where $n$ is the number we are calculating the factorial of. Given $n = 4$, for example, this gives:

```
(Y G) 4
G (Y G) 4
(λr.λn.(1, if n = 0; else n × (r (n−1)))) (Y G) 4
(λn.(1, if n = 0; else n × ((Y G) (n−1)))) 4
1, if 4 = 0; else 4 × ((Y G) (4−1))
4 × (G (Y G) (4−1))
4 × ((λn.(1, if n = 0; else n × ((Y G) (n−1)))) (4−1))
4 × (1, if 3 = 0; else 3 × ((Y G) (3−1)))
4 × (3 × (G (Y G) (3−1)))
4 × (3 × ((λn.(1, if n = 0; else n × ((Y G) (n−1)))) (3−1)))
4 × (3 × (1, if 2 = 0; else 2 × ((Y G) (2−1))))
4 × (3 × (2 × (G (Y G) (2−1))))
4 × (3 × (2 × ((λn.(1, if n = 0; else n × ((Y G) (n−1)))) (2−1))))
4 × (3 × (2 × (1, if 1 = 0; else 1 × ((Y G) (1−1)))))
4 × (3 × (2 × (1 × (G (Y G) (1−1)))))
4 × (3 × (2 × (1 × ((λn.(1, if n = 0; else n × ((Y G) (n−1)))) (1−1)))))
4 × (3 × (2 × (1 × (1, if 0 = 0; else 0 × ((Y G) (0−1))))))
4 × (3 × (2 × (1 × (1))))
24
```

Every recursively defined function can be seen as a fixed point of some suitably-defined function closing over the recursive call with an extra argument, and therefore, using **Y**, every recursively defined function can be expressed as a lambda expression. In particular, we can now cleanly define the subtraction, multiplication and comparison predicate of natural numbers recursively.

## Standard terms

Certain terms have commonly accepted names:

```
I := λx.x
K := λx.λy.x
S := λx.λy.λz.x z (y z)
ω := λx.x x
Ω := ω ω
Y := λg.(λx.g (x x)) (λx.g (x x))
```

## Computable functions and lambda calculus

A function $F: \mathbf{N} \to \mathbf{N}$ of natural numbers is a computable function if and only if there exists a lambda expression $f$ such that for every pair of $x$, $y$ in $\mathbf{N}$, $F(x)=y$ if and only if $f\ x =_\beta y$, where $x$ and $y$ are the Church numerals corresponding to $x$ and $y$, respectively and $=_\beta$ meaning equivalence with beta reduction. This is one of the many ways to define computability; see the Church-Turing thesis for a discussion of other approaches and their equivalence.

## Undecidability of equivalence

There is no algorithm that takes as input two lambda expressions and outputs TRUE or FALSE depending on whether or not the two expressions are equivalent. This was historically the first problem for which undecidability could be proven. As is common for a proof of undecidability, the proof shows that no computable function can decide the equivalence. Church's thesis is then invoked to show that no algorithm can do so.

Church's proof first reduces the problem to determining whether a given lambda expression has a *normal form*. A normal form is an equivalent expression that cannot be reduced any further under the rules imposed by the form. Then he assumes that this predicate is computable, and can hence be expressed in lambda calculus. Building on earlier work by Kleene and constructing a Gödel numbering for lambda expressions, he constructs a lambda expression $e$ that closely follows the proof of Gödel's first incompleteness theorem. If $e$ is applied to its own Gödel number, a contradiction results.

## Lambda calculus and programming languages

As pointed out by Peter Landin's 1965 paper A Correspondence between ALGOL 60 and Church's Lambda-notation [14], sequential procedural programming languages can be understood in terms of the lambda calculus, which provides the basic mechanisms for procedural abstraction and procedure (subprogram) application.

Lambda calculus reifies "functions" and makes them first-class objects, which raises implementation complexity when it is implemented.

### First-class functions

Further information: First-class function and Anonymous function

For example in Lisp the 'square' function can be expressed as a lambda expression as follows:

```
(lambda (x) (* x x))
```

or the same expressed in Haskell:

```
\x -> x*x -- where the \ denotes the greek λ
```

The above example is an expression that evaluates to a first-class function. The symbol lambda creates an anonymous function, given a list of parameter names, (x) — just a single argument in this case, and an expression that is evaluated as the body of the function, (* x x). The Haskell example is identical. Anonymous functions are sometimes called lambda expressions.

For example Pascal and many other imperative languages have long supported passing subprograms as arguments to other subprograms through the mechanism of function pointers. However, function pointers are not sufficient condition for functions to be first class datatype because if and only if new instances of a function can be created at run time, the functions are first class datatype. And this run-time creation of functions is supported in C++, Smalltalk, and more recently in Scala, Eiffel ("agents") and C# ("delegates"), among others.

Below is an example expressed as the Eiffel "inline agent"

```
agent (x: REAL): REAL do Result := x * x end
```

The object corresponds to the lambda expression λx.x*x (with call by value) because it can be assigned to a variable or passed around to routines, i.e. treated like any other expression.

A Python example of this uses the lambda [15] form of functions:

```
func = lambda x: x ** 2
```

This creates a new anonymous function and names it **func** that can be passed to other functions, stored in variables, etc. Python can also treat any other function created with the standard def [16] statement as first-class objects.

The same holds for Smalltalk expression

```
[ :x | x * x ]
```

This is first-class object (block closure), which can be stored in variables, passed as arguments, etc.

A similar expression using C++11 anonymous function, but specifically for integers, is:

```
[] (int i) -> int { return i * i; }
```

In JavaScript since version 1.8, the notation:

```
function(x) x*x;
```

is used. In older versions

```
function(x) { return x*x; }
```

In Scala:

```
(x:Int) => x*x
```

In F#:

```
(fun x -> x * x)
```

In D:

```
x => x * x         // when parameter type can be inferred
(int x) => x * x   // when parameter type must be specified
```

## Reduction strategies

Whether a term is normalising or not, and how much work needs to be done in normalising it if it is, depends to a large extent on the reduction strategy used. The distinction between reduction strategies relates to the distinction in functional programming languages between eager evaluation and lazy evaluation.

Full beta reductions

> Any redex can be reduced at any time. This means essentially the lack of any particular reduction strategy—with regard to reducibility, "all bets are off".

Applicative order

> The rightmost, innermost redex is always reduced first. Intuitively this means a function's arguments are always reduced before the function itself. Applicative order always attempts to apply functions to normal forms, even when this is not possible.

> Most programming languages (including Lisp, ML and imperative languages like C and Java) are described as "strict", meaning that functions applied to non-normalising arguments are non-normalising. This is done essentially using applicative order, call by value reduction (see below), but usually called "eager evaluation".

Normal order

The leftmost, outermost redex is always reduced first. That is, whenever possible the arguments are substituted into the body of an abstraction before the arguments are reduced.

Call by name

As normal order, but no reductions are performed inside abstractions. For example $\lambda x.\,(\lambda x.x)\,x$ is in normal form according to this strategy, although it contains the redex $(\lambda x.x)\,x$.

Call by value

Only the outermost redexes are reduced: a redex is reduced only when its right hand side has reduced to a value (variable or lambda abstraction).

Call by need

As normal order, but function applications that would duplicate terms instead name the argument, which is then reduced only "when it is needed". Called in practical contexts "lazy evaluation". In implementations this "name" takes the form of a pointer, with the redex represented by a thunk.

Applicative order is not a normalising strategy. The usual counterexample is as follows: define $\Omega$ = $\omega\omega$ where $\omega$ = $\lambda x.xx$. This entire expression contains only one redex, namely the whole expression; its reduct is again $\Omega$. Since this is the only available reduction, $\Omega$ has no normal form (under any evaluation strategy). Using applicative order, the expression $\mathbf{KI\Omega}$ = $(\lambda x.\lambda y.x)$ $(\lambda x.x)\,\Omega$ is reduced by first reducing $\Omega$ to normal form (since it is the rightmost redex), but since $\Omega$ has no normal form, applicative order fails to find a normal form for $\mathbf{KI\Omega}$.

In contrast, normal order is so called because it always finds a normalising reduction, if one exists. In the above example, $\mathbf{KI\Omega}$ reduces under normal order to $I$, a normal form. A drawback is that redexes in the arguments may be copied, resulting in duplicated computation (for example, $(\lambda x.xx)$ $((\lambda x.x)\,y)$ reduces to $((\lambda x.x)\,y)$ $((\lambda x.x)\,y)$ using this strategy; now there are two redexes, so full evaluation needs two more steps, but if the argument had been reduced first, there would now be none).

The positive tradeoff of using applicative order is that it does not cause unnecessary computation, if all arguments are used, because it never substitutes arguments containing redexes and hence never needs to copy them (which would duplicate work). In the above example, in applicative order $(\lambda x.xx)$ $((\lambda x.x)\,y)$ reduces first to $(\lambda x.xx)\,y$ and then to the normal order $yy$, taking two steps instead of three.

Most *purely* functional programming languages (notably Miranda and its descendents, including Haskell), and the proof languages of theorem provers, use *lazy evaluation*, which is essentially the same as call by need. This is like normal order reduction, but call by need manages to avoid the duplication of work inherent in normal order reduction using *sharing*. In the example given above, $(\lambda x.xx)$ $((\lambda x.x)\,y)$ reduces to $((\lambda x.x)\,y)$ $((\lambda x.x)\,y)$, which has two redexes, but in call by need they are represented using the same object rather than copied, so when one is reduced the other is too.

## A note about complexity

While the idea of beta reduction seems simple enough, it is not an atomic step, in that it must have a non-trivial cost when estimating computational complexity.[17] To be precise, one must somehow find the location of all of the occurrences of the bound variable $V$ in the expression $E$, implying a time cost, or one must keep track of these locations in some way, implying a space cost. A naïve search for the locations of $V$ in $E$ is $O(n)$ in the length $n$ of $E$. This has led to the study of systems that use explicit substitution. Sinot's director strings[18] offer a way of tracking the locations of free variables in expressions.

## Parallelism and concurrency

The Church-Rosser property of the lambda calculus means that evaluation (β-reduction) can be carried out in *any order*, even in parallel. This means that various nondeterministic evaluation strategies are relevant. However, the lambda calculus does not offer any explicit constructs for parallelism. One can add constructs such as Futures to the lambda calculus. Other process calculi have been developed for describing communication and concurrency.

# Semantics

The fact that lambda calculus terms act as functions on other lambda calculus terms, and even on themselves, led to questions about the semantics of the lambda calculus. Could a sensible meaning be assigned to lambda calculus terms? The natural semantics was to find a set $D$ isomorphic to the function space $D \to D$, of functions on itself. However, no nontrivial such $D$ can exist, by cardinality constraints because the set of all functions from $D$ into $D$ has greater cardinality than $D$.

In the 1970s, Dana Scott showed that, if only continuous functions were considered, a set or domain $D$ with the required property could be found, thus providing a model for the lambda calculus.

This work also formed the basis for the denotational semantics of programming languages.

# See also

- Applicative computing systems – Treatment of objects in the style of the lambda calculus
- Binary Lambda Calculus – A version of lambda calculus with binary I/O, a binary encoding of terms, and a designated universal machine.
- Calculus of constructions – A typed lambda calculus with types as first-class values
- Cartesian closed category – A setting for lambda calculus in category theory
- Categorical abstract machine – A model of computation applicable to lambda calculus
- Combinatory logic – A notation for mathematical logic without variables
- Curry–Howard isomorphism – The formal correspondence between programs and proofs
- Domain theory – Study of certain posets giving denotational semantics for lambda calculus
- Evaluation strategy – Rules for the evaluation of expressions in programming languages
- Explicit substitution – The theory of substitution, as used in β-reduction
- Harrop formula – A kind of constructive logical formula such that proofs are lambda terms
- Kappa calculus – A first-order analogue of lambda calculus
- Kleene–Rosser paradox – A demonstration that some form of lambda calculus is inconsistent
- Knights of the Lambda Calculus – A semi-fictional organization of LISP and Scheme hackers
- Lambda cube – A framework for some extensions of typed lambda calculus
- Lambda-mu calculus – An extension of the lambda calculus for treating classical logic
- Rewriting – Transformation of formulæ in formal systems
- SECD machine – A virtual machine designed for the lambda calculus
- Simply typed lambda calculus - Version(s) with a single type constructor
- SKI combinator calculus – A computational system based on the **S**, **K** and **I** combinators
- System F – A typed lambda calculus with type-variables
- Typed lambda calculus – Lambda calculus with typed variables (and functions)
- Universal Turing machine – A formal computing machine that is equivalent to lambda calculus
- Unlambda – An esoteric functional programming language based on combinatory logic

# References

[1]  A. Church, "A set of postulates for the foundation of logic", *Annals of Mathematics*, Series 2, 33:346–366 (1932).

[2]  For a full history, see Cardone and Hindley's "History of Lambda-calculus and Combinatory Logic" (2006).

[3]  A. Church, "An unsolvable problem of elementary number theory", *American Journal of Mathematics*, Volume 58, No. 2. (April 1936), pp. 345-363.

[4]  A. Church, "A Formulation of the Simple Theory of Types", *Journal of Symbolic Logic*, Volume 5 (1940).

[5]  Barendregt, Hendrik Pieter (1984), *The Lambda Calculus: Its Syntax and Semantics* (http://www.elsevier.com/wps/find/bookdescription. cws_home/501727/description), Studies in Logic and the Foundations of Mathematics, **103** (Revised ed.), North Holland, Amsterdam. Corrections (ftp://ftp.cs.ru.nl/pub/CompMath.Found/ErrataLCalculus.pdf), ISBN 0-444-87508-5,

[6]  Example for Rules of Associativity (http://www.lambda-bound.com/book/lambdacalc/node27.html)

[7]  Selinger, Peter, *Lecture Notes on the Lambda Calculus* (http://www.mathstat.dal.ca/~selinger/papers/lambdanotes.pdf), Department of Mathematics and Statistics, University of Ottawa, pp. 9,

[8]  Example for Rule of Associativity (http://www.lambda-bound.com/book/lambdacalc/node25.html)

[9]  Barendregt, Henk; Barendsen, Erik (March 2000), *Introduction to Lambda Calculus* (ftp://ftp.cs.ru.nl/pub/CompMath.Found/lambda. pdf),

[10]  de Queiroz, Ruy J.G.B. " A Proof-Theoretic Account of Programming and the Role of Reduction Rules. (http://dx.doi.org/10.1111/j. 1746-8361.1988.tb00919.x)" *Dialectica* **42**(4), pages 265-282, 1988.

[11]  Turbak, Franklyn; Gifford, David (2008), *Design concepts in programming languages*, MIT press, p. 251, ISBN 9780262201759

[12]  Felleisen, Matthias; Flatt, Matthew (2006), *Programming Languages and Lambda Calculi* (http://www.cs.utah.edu/plt/publications/ pllc.pdf), pp. 26,

[13]  Selinger, Peter, *Lecture Notes on the Lambda Calculus* (http://www.mathstat.dal.ca/~selinger/papers/lambdanotes.pdf), Department of Mathematics and Statistics, University of Ottawa, pp. 16,

[14]  http://portal.acm.org/citation.cfm?id=363749&coll=portal&dl=ACM

[15]  http://docs.python.org/ref/lambdas.html#lambda

[16]  http://docs.python.org/ref/function.html

[17]  R. Statman, " The typed λ-calculus is not elementary recursive. (http://ieeexplore.ieee.org/xpl/freeabs_all.jsp?arnumber=4567929)" *Theoretical Computer Science*, (1979) **9** pp73-81.

[18]  F.-R. Sinot. " Director Strings Revisited: A Generic Approach to the Efficient Representation of Free Variables in Higher-order Rewriting. (http://www.lsv.ens-cachan.fr/~sinot/publis.php?onlykey=sinot-jlc05)" *Journal of Logic and Computation* **15**(2), pages 201-218, 2005.

# Further reading

- Abelson, Harold & Gerald Jay Sussman. Structure and Interpretation of Computer Programs. The MIT Press. ISBN 0-262-51087-1.

- Hendrik Pieter Barendregt *Introduction to Lambda Calculus* (ftp://ftp.cs.ru.nl/pub/CompMath.Found/ lambda.pdf).

- Henk Barendregt, The Impact of the Lambda Calculus in Logic and Computer Science (http://people.emich. edu/pstephen/other_papers/Impact of the Lambda Calculus.pdf). The Bulletin of Symbolic Logic, Volume 3, Number 2, June 1997.

- Barendregt, Hendrik Pieter, *The Type Free Lambda Calculus* pp1091–1132 of *Handbook of Mathematical Logic*, North-Holland (1977) ISBN 0-7204-2285-X

- Cardone and Hindley, 2006. History of Lambda-calculus and Combinatory Logic (http://www-maths.swan.ac. uk/staff/jrh/papers/JRHHislamWeb.pdf). In Gabbay and Woods (eds.), *Handbook of the History of Logic*, vol. 5. Elsevier.

- Church, Alonzo, *An unsolvable problem of elementary number theory*, American Journal of Mathematics, 58 (1936), pp. 345–363. This paper contains the proof that the equivalence of lambda expressions is in general not decidable.

- Kleene, Stephen, *A theory of positive integers in formal logic*, American Journal of Mathematics, 57 (1935), pp. 153–173 and 219–244. Contains the lambda calculus definitions of several familiar functions.

- Landin, Peter, *A Correspondence Between ALGOL 60 and Church's Lambda-Notation*, Communications of the ACM, vol. 8, no. 2 (1965), pages 89–101. Available from the ACM site (http://portal.acm.org/citation. cfm?id=363749&coll=portal&dl=ACM). A classic paper highlighting the importance of lambda calculus as a basis for programming languages.

- Larson, Jim, *An Introduction to Lambda Calculus and Scheme* (http://www.jetcafe.org/~jim/lambda.html). A gentle introduction for programmers.
- Schalk, A. and Simmons, H. (2005) *An introduction to λ-calculi and arithmetic with a decent selection of exercises* (http://www.cs.man.ac.uk/~hsimmons/BOOKS/lcalculus.pdf). *Notes for a course in the Mathematical Logic MSc at Manchester University.*
- de Queiroz, Ruy J.G.B. (2008) *On Reduction Rules, Meaning-as-Use and Proof-Theoretic Semantics* (http://www.springerlink.com/content/27nk266126k817gq/). Studia Logica, 90(2):211-247. A paper giving a formal underpinning to the idea of 'meaning-is-use' which, even if based on proofs, it is different from proof-theoretic semantics as in the Dummett–Prawitz tradition since it takes reduction as the rules giving meaning.

Monographs/textbooks for graduate students:

- Morten Heine Sørensen, Paweł Urzyczyn, *Lectures on the Curry-Howard isomorphism*, Elsevier, 2006, ISBN 0-444-52077-5 is a recent monograph that covers the main topics of lambda calculus from the type-free variety, to most typed lambda calculi, including more recent developments like pure type systems and the lambda cube. It does not cover subtyping extensions.
- Pierce, Benjamin (2002), *Types and Programming Languages*, MIT Press, ISBN 0-262-16209-1 covers lambda calculi from a practical type system perspective; some topics like dependent types are only mentioned, but subtyping is an important topic.

*Some parts of this article are based on material from FOLDOC, used with permission.*

# External links

- Achim Jung, *A Short Introduction to the Lambda Calculus* (http://www.cs.bham.ac.uk/~axj/pub/papers/lambda-calculus.pdf)-(PDF)
- David C. Keenan, *To Dissect a Mockingbird: A Graphical Notation for the Lambda Calculus with Animated Reduction* (http://dkeenan.com/Lambda/)
- Raúl Rojas, *A Tutorial Introduction to the Lambda Calculus* (http://www.inf.fu-berlin.de/lehre/WS03/alpi/lambda.pdf)-(PDF)
- Peter Selinger, *Lecture Notes on the Lambda Calculus* (http://www.mscs.dal.ca/~selinger/papers/#lambdanotes)-(PDF)
- L. Allison, *Some executable λ-calculus examples* (http://www.allisons.org/ll/FP/Lambda/Examples/)
- Georg P. Loczewski, *The Lambda Calculus and A++* (http://www.lambda-bound.com/book/lambdacalc/lcalconl.html)
- Bret Victor, *Alligator Eggs: A Puzzle Game Based on Lambda Calculus* (http://worrydream.com/AlligatorEggs/)
- *Lambda Calculus* (http://www.safalra.com/science/lambda-calculus/) on Safalra's Website (http://www.safalra.com/)
- *Lambda Calculus* (http://planetmath.org/?op=getobj&from=objects&id=2788), *PlanetMath.org.*
- LCI Lambda Interpreter (http://lci.sourceforge.net/) a simple yet powerful pure calculus interpreter
- Lambda Calculus links on Lambda-the-Ultimate (http://lambda-the-ultimate.org/classic/lc.html)
- Mike Thyer, Lambda Animator (http://thyer.name/lambda-animator/), a graphical Java applet demonstrating alternative reduction strategies.
- An Introduction to Lambda Calculus and Scheme (http://www.jetcafe.org/~jim/lambda.html), by Jim Larson

# Article Sources and Contributors

**Denotational_semantics_of_the_Actor_model** *Source*: http://en.wikipedia.org/w/index.php?title=Denotational_semantics_of_the_Actor_model *Contributors*: Allan McInnes, Anonymouser, Bakineggs, Blaisorblade, Booyabazooka, CBM, CarlHewitt, Charles Matthews, David Humphreys, Enoksrd, Garion96, Jpbowen, Madmardigan53, Miym, Salix alba, Sam Staton, 28 anonymous edits

**Denotational_semantics** *Source*: http://en.wikipedia.org/w/index.php?title=Denotational_semantics *Contributors*: 2ndMouse, Abcarter, Allan McInnes, Andrewbirkett, Andycjp, Anonymouser, Artem M. Pelenitsyn, Basploeger, Beetstra, Bosmon, Bramschoenmakers, Brighterorange, CBM, Camrn86, CarlHewitt, Catamorphism, Cdibuduo, Ceyockey, Chalst, Charles Matthews, Cmdrjameson, Cybercobra, Dabomb87, David Eppstein, David Humphreys, GB fan, Gauge, Grshiplett, Hairy Dude, Hpvpp, Hqb, J2thawiki, Jpbowen, Jrincayc, Knotwork, Koffieyahoo, LOL, Leibniz, Lightmouse, Linas, Macrakis, Madmediamaven, Marudubshinki, MathMartin, Mhss, Michael Hardy, Mild Bill Hiccup, Miym, Neilc, Oleg Alexandrov, PJTraill, Pcap, Physis, Rich Farmbrough, Rursus, Ruud Koot, Salix alba, Sam Staton, Slaniel, Smimram, TakuyaMurata, The Anome, TheParanoidOne, Thv, Tressider, TuukkaH, Uninverted, Van der Hoorn, Vkuncak, 125 anonymous edits

**Domain_theory** *Source*: http://en.wikipedia.org/w/index.php?title=Domain_theory *Contributors*: Axlle, Bethnim, BrEyes, CarlHewitt, Charles Matthews, Charvest, Crystallina, Cybercobra, Dfletter, Dominus, Elwikipedista, Erxnmedia, FF2010, Ferkelparade, Frege, Gandalf61, Hairy Dude, Hike395, Inquam, Japanese Searobin, Jeff3000, Jpbowen, Kbdank71, Kell, Koffieyahoo, Leibniz, Magmi, Malcohol, Markus Krötzsch, Mets501, Mhss, Michael Hardy, Msh210, Novacatz, Oleg Alexandrov, Physis, Plmday, QplQyer, Ruud Koot, ST47, Salasks, Sam Staton, Suisui, Tobias Bergemann, Undsoweiter, Vdamanafshan, Zaslav, 48 anonymous edits

**Actor_model** *Source*: http://en.wikipedia.org/w/index.php?title=Actor_model *Contributors*: AgadaUrbanit, Allan McInnes, AmigoNico, Angus Lepper, Anonymouser, ArthurDenture, Arthuredelstein, Attys, BMF81, Beef, Ben Standeven, Bobo192, Bombnumber20, CBM, CSTAR, CanadianLinuxUser, CarlHewitt, Cfeet77, Cmdrjameson, Cosmotron, Cxbrx, DNewhall, David Humphreys, David-Sarah Hopwood, DerHexer, Dibblego, Dleonard, Donhalcon, Dougher, DuncanCragg, Ems57fcva, FatalError, Finlay McWalter, FrankSanMiguel, Fresheneesz, Gauge, Gracefool, Guy Harris, Hairy Dude, Hillman, History2007, Hoodow, Indil, Jack Waugh, Janm67, Jantangring, Jkeene, Jodal, Jonasboner, Joris.deguet, Josh Parris, Joswig, Jpbowen, Junkblocker, Karol Langner, Kku, Knotwork, Koffieyahoo, Kpalsson, Kthejoker, Kusma, La goutte de pluie, Laforge49, Linas, Llywrch, Lradrama, Lunalot, Madair, Madmediamaven, Magicmonster, Marudubshinki, Mboverload, Michael Hardy, Mimi.vx, Mipadi, Modify, Necromantiarian, Ojw, Oli Filth, Oluies, Orthologist, Peterdjones, Pgan002, Piet Delport, PoweredByLolcats, Prof. Hewitt, Ptrelford, Pxma, Qwertyus, Rabarberski, Ravn, Rijkbenik, Rivimey, Rjwilmsi, Rkumar8, RobinMessage, Rohan Jayasekera, Ruud Koot, Ryan Roos, Sam Pointon, Sam Staton, Samsara, SarekOfVulcan, Shanewholloway, Sietse Snel, SimonP, Slicky, SpuriousQ, Sstrader, Stevedekorte, Stuart Morrow, TRBP, Tajmiester, Tbhotch, Terryn3, Texture, TimBentley, Tobias Bergemann, Tony Sidaway, Tonyrex, Torc2, Trevyn, Untalker, Vonkje, Wbm1058, Welsh, Worrydream, Xaliqen, Xan2, Xaonon, 267 anonymous edits

**Partially_ordered_set** *Source*: http://en.wikipedia.org/w/index.php?title=Partially_ordered_set *Contributors*: Ankan babee, Arcfrk, AugPi, Bcrowell, Bissinger, Brick Thrower, BrotherE, Bryan Derksen, CBM, CRGreathouse, Cesine, Charles Matthews, Cheesefondue, Chinju, ComputerGeezer, Confluente, Conversion script, David Eppstein, David-Sarah Hopwood, DefLog, Digby Tantrum, Dmharvey, DougOrleans, Dysprosia, Esoth, Fibonacci, Fropuff, GTBacchus, GaborLajos, Giftlite, Gnathan87, Gubbubu, Haham hanuka, Hans Adler, Haseldon, Helder.wiki, IdealOmniscience, Ill logic, Jakshap, Javalenok, Jcarroll, Jdthood, Jludwig, Justin W Smith, Kilom691, Kjetil1001, L'œuf, Laurentius, Lipedia, Luckyz, MFH, Marc van Leeuwen, MarkSweep, Markus Krötzsch, Maximus Rex, Megaloxantha, Methossant, Mike Fikes, Morinus, Msh210, Nbarth, Neilc, Oleg Alexandrov, Orphic, Palnot, Patrick, Paul August, PaulTanenbaum, Peiresc, Peruvianllama, Pi zero, Porton, RDBury, Rathgemz, Ricardo Ferreira de Oliveira, Rlupsa, RobertDanielEmerson, Salix alba, Sanguinity, Setitup, SlamDiego, Spoon!, SteveWoolf, TakuyaMurata, Tbleher, The man who was Friday, TheGhostOfAdrianMineha, TheJames, Thecheesykid, Thehotelambush, Throw it in the Fire, Timwi, Tobias Bergemann, Tomo, Undsoweiter, Urhixidur, Vaughan Pratt, Vdamanafshan, Vecter, Vonkje, Werratal, Zaslav, Zundark, 76 anonymous edits

**Indeterminacy_in_concurrent_computation** *Source*: http://en.wikipedia.org/w/index.php?title=Indeterminacy_in_concurrent_computation *Contributors*: 2ndMouse, Allan McInnes, Arthur Rubin, Ben Standeven, Blaisorblade, Bunkar, CBM, CSTAR, CarlHewitt, Charles Matthews, DéRahier, Ems57fcva, Gauge, Giftlite, Janm67, Joeblakesley, Jpbowen, Koffieyahoo, LWG, Linas, Marudubshinki, Neutral current, Qwertzy2, Rich Farmbrough, Shimonnyman, Uncle G, 8 anonymous edits

**Lambda_calculus** *Source*: http://en.wikipedia.org/w/index.php?title=Lambda_calculus *Contributors*: 195.166.58.xxx, A3 nm, Abcarter, Adamuu, Adrianwn, Aeris-chan, Afarnen, AmigoNico, Ancheta Wis, Andre Engels, AndreasBWagner, AnnaFrance, Antonielly, Apokrif, Ariovistus, Artem M. Pelenitsyn, Arvindn, AugPi, Awegmann, AxelBoldt, Bbpen, BeastRHIT, Bfreis, BiT, Blaisorblade, BlakeStone, Bryan Derksen, Bsmntbombdood, Burritoburritoburrito, CBM, CLW, CLeJ37, CYD, CarlHewitt, CeilingCrash, Centrx, Chalst, Charles Matthews, Chbarts, Cinayakoshka, Classicalecon, Cmdrjameson, ComputScientist, Conversion script, Corti, Cyp, D.keenan, DPMulligan, DancingPhilosopher, Daniel.Cardenas, Daniel5Ko, David Gerard, Dcattell, Dddenton, Demosthenes2k8, Derek Ross, Dfletter, Diego Moya, Dominus, Donhalcon, Dratman, Dreamyshade, Dreblen, Dwiddows, Dysprosia, Edinwiki, Elwikipedista, Enisbayramoglu, EoGuy, Equilibrioception, Eric119, Esap, Evaluist, EvanSeeds, Everyking, Evil Monkey, Ffangs, FiP, Fubar Obfusco, Fuchsias, Furrykef, Future ahead, GTBacchus, Gabn1, General Wesc, Giftlite, Gioto, Glacialfox, GlassFET, Glenn, GoatGuy, Gploc, Gpvos, GrdScarabe, Gregbard, GregorB, Gruu, Hairy Dude, Hakeem.gadi, Hans Adler, Henk Barendregt, Herbee, Hmains, Holoed, Hooperbloob, HowardBGolden, Ht686rg90, Hugo Herbelin, Hyh1048576, Idmillington, Illpoint, Iridescence, Iridescent, Ironrange, J.Dong820, JLaTondre, JMK, Jacob Finn, James Crippen, JamieVicary, Jan Hidders, Jason Quinn, Jesin, Jimmyzimms, Jleedev, Joel7687, John Baez, John Millikin, John Vandenberg, Jonabbey, Jonas, Jonas AGX, Jorend, Joswig, Joy, Jpbowen, Jtbandes, JulesH, Jyavner, Jyossarian, KHamsun, Kallocain, Karl Dickman, Karun.mahajan, Keenan Pepper, Kensai, Khukri, Kirk Hilliard, Kizeral, Koffieyahoo, Kowey, Krauss, Kripkenstein, Kwantus, LC, LOL, Lambiam, Lance Williams, Landon1980, Largoplazo, Lawandeconomics1, Leibniz, Lexspoon, Linas, Liyang, Lloyd, Longratana, LunaticFringe, MBParker, MBisanz, MH, Makkuro, Malcohol, Maniac18, MarSch, Markhurd, Marudubshinki, MathKnight, MathMartin, Matt McIrvin, MattGiuca, Mattc58, Mcaruso, Mcld, Meiskam, Mets501, Michael Hardy, Michael Slone, Minesweeper, Morgaladh, Mormegil, Ms2ger, Msreeharsha, N5iln, Nanshu, Natkuhn, Nczempin, Neelix, Neilc, NewEnglandYankee, Noamz, Nomeata, Nonlinear149, Nowhere man, Numl0k, Oleg Alexandrov, OlegAndreev, PJTraill, Paul Richter, Pcap, Pedzsan, Pekinensis, PenguiN42, Physis, Piast93, Pinethicket, Pintman, Pjvpjv, Pmronchi, Populus, Potatoswatter, Punto7, Pyrop, Qwertyus, Qwfp, R'n'B, R.e.s., Radagast3, Raise exception, Rearete, ResearchRave, Rich Farmbrough, Roaryk, Roccorossi, Royote, Ruud Koot, Sae1962, Sam Pointon, Sam Staton, Sanspeur, Sarex, Saric, ScottBurson, Serhei Makarov, Shades79, Sherjilozair, Shredderyin, Siafu, Sligocki, Slipstream, Smack, Softtest123, Some jerk on the Internet, Spiff, Stanmanish, StevenDH, StevenDaryl, Stratocracy, TehKeg, TelecomNut, TenOfAllTrades, The Anome, The Thing That Should Not Be, Theone256, Thryduulf, Thunderforge, Tigrisek, Tim Retout, Timwi, Titoxd, Tobias Bergemann, Tobias Hoevekamp, Tomchiukc, Tony Sidaway, Torc2, Tromp, Trueyoutrueme, TypesGuy1234, Ultra two, Urhixidur, VKokielov, Vadmium, Valeria.depaiva, Vcunat, Vegaswikian, Venullian, Vonkje, Vulture, WLoku, Wafulz, Wanze, Wedesoft, Wgunther, Whiteknox, WillNess, Wknight94, Workaphobia, WuTheFWasThat, Zaheen, Zero sharp, ZeroOne, Zygmunt lozinski, Пика Пика, 461 anonymous edits

# Image Sources, Licenses and Contributors

**Image:Hasse diagram of powerset of 3.svg** *Source*: http://en.wikipedia.org/w/index.php?title=File:Hasse_diagram_of_powerset_of_3.svg *License*: unknown *Contributors*: User:KSmrq

**Image:poset6.jpg** *Source*: http://en.wikipedia.org/w/index.php?title=File:Poset6.jpg *License*: unknown *Contributors*: Bkell, Cesine

GNU Free Documentation License Version 1.2, November 2002 Copyright (C) 2000,2001,2002 Free Software Foundation, Inc. 59 Temple Place, Suite 330, Boston, MA 02111-1307 USA Everyone is permitted to copy and distribute verbatim copies of this license document, but changing it is not allowed.

0. PREAMBLE
The purpose of this License is to make a manual, textbook, or other functional and useful document "free" in the sense of freedom: to assure everyone the effective freedom to copy and redistribute it, with or without modifying it, either commercially or noncommercially. Secondarily, this License preserves for the author and publisher a way to get credit for their work, while not being considered responsible for modifications made by others. This License is a kind of "copyleft", which means that derivative works of the document must themselves be free in the same sense. It complements the GNU General Public License, which is a copyleft license designed for free software. We have designed this License in order to use it for manuals for free software, because free software needs free documentation: a free program should come with manuals providing the same freedoms that the software does. But this License is not limited to software manuals; it can be used for any textual work, regardless of subject matter or whether it is published as a printed book. We recommend this License principally for works whose purpose is instruction or reference.

1. APPLICABILITY AND DEFINITIONS
This License applies to any manual or other work, in any medium, that contains a notice placed by the copyright holder saying it can be distributed under the terms of this License. Such a notice grants a world-wide, royalty-free license, unlimited in duration, to use that work under the conditions stated herein. The "Document", below, refers to any such manual or work. Any member of the public is a licensee, and is addressed as "you". You accept the license if you copy, modify or distribute the work in a way requiring permission under copyright law. A "Modified Version" of the Document means any work containing the Document or a portion of it, either copied verbatim, or with modifications and/or translated into another language. A "Secondary Section" is a named appendix or a front-matter section of the Document that deals exclusively with the relationship of the publishers or authors of the Document to the Document's overall subject (or to related matters) and contains nothing that could fall directly within that overall subject. (Thus, if the Document is in part a textbook of mathematics, a Secondary Section may not explain any mathematics.) The relationship could be a matter of historical connection with the subject or with related matters, or of legal, commercial, philosophical, ethical or political position regarding them. The "Invariant Sections" are certain Secondary Sections whose titles are designated, as being those of Invariant Sections, in the notice that says that the Document is released under this License. If a section does not fit the above definition of Secondary then it is not allowed to be designated as Invariant. The Document may contain zero Invariant Sections. If the Document does not identify any Invariant Sections then there are none. The "Cover Texts" are certain short passages of text that are listed, as Front-Cover Texts or Back-Cover Texts, in the notice that says that the Document is released under this License. A Front-Cover Text may be at most 5 words, and a Back-Cover Text may be at most 25 words. A "Transparent" copy of the Document means a machine-readable copy, represented in a format whose specification is available to the general public, that is suitable for revising the document straightforwardly with generic text editors or (for images composed of pixels) generic paint programs or (for drawings) some widely available drawing editor, and that is suitable for input to text formatters or for automatic translation to a variety of formats suitable for input to text formatters. A copy made in an otherwise Transparent file format whose markup, or absence of markup, has been arranged to thwart or discourage subsequent modification by readers is not Transparent. An image format is not Transparent if used for any substantial amount of text. A copy that is not "Transparent" is called "Opaque". Examples of suitable formats for Transparent copies include plain ASCII without markup, Texinfo input format, LaTeX input format, SGML or XML using a publicly available DTD, and standard-conforming simple HTML, PostScript or PDF designed for human modification. Examples of transparent image formats include PNG, XCF and JPG. Opaque formats include proprietary formats that can be read and edited only by proprietary word processors, SGML or XML for which the DTD and/or processing tools are not generally available, and the machine-generated HTML, PostScript or PDF produced by some word processors for output purposes only. The "Title Page" means, for a printed book, the title page itself, plus such following pages as are needed to hold, legibly, the material this License requires to appear in the title page. For works in formats which do not have any title page as such, "Title Page" means the text near the most prominent appearance of the work's title, preceding the beginning of the body of the text. A section "Entitled XYZ" means a named subunit of the Document whose title either is precisely XYZ or contains XYZ in parentheses following text that translates XYZ in another language. (Here XYZ stands for a specific section name mentioned below, such as "Acknowledgements", "Dedications", "Endorsements", or "History".) To "Preserve the Title" of such a section when you modify the Document means that it remains a section "Entitled XYZ" according to this definition. The Document may include Warranty Disclaimers next to the notice which states that this License applies to the Document. These Warranty Disclaimers are considered to be included by reference in this License, but only as regards disclaiming warranties: any other implication that these Warranty Disclaimers may have is void and has no effect on the meaning of this License.

2. VERBATIM COPYING
You may copy and distribute the Document in any medium, either commercially or noncommercially, provided that this License, the copyright notices, and the license notice saying this License applies to the Document are reproduced in all copies, and that you add no other conditions whatsoever to those of this License. You may not use technical measures to obstruct or control the reading or further copying of the copies you make or distribute. However, you may accept compensation in exchange for copies. If you distribute a large enough number of copies you must also follow the conditions in section 3. You may also lend copies, under the same conditions stated above, and you may publicly display copies.

3. COPYING IN QUANTITY
If you publish printed copies (or copies in media that commonly have printed covers) of the Document, numbering more than 100, and the Document's license notice requires Cover Texts, you must enclose the copies in covers that carry, clearly and legibly, all these Cover Texts: Front-Cover Texts on the front cover, and Back-Cover Texts on the back cover. Both covers must also clearly and legibly identify you as the publisher of these copies. The front cover must present the full title with all words of the title equally prominent and visible. You may add other material on the covers in addition. Copying with changes limited to the covers, as long as they preserve the title of the Document and satisfy these conditions, can be treated as verbatim copying in other respects. If the required texts for either cover are too voluminous to fit legibly, you should put the first ones listed (as many as fit reasonably) on the actual cover, and continue the rest onto adjacent pages. If you publish or distribute Opaque copies of the Document numbering more than 100, you must either include a machine-readable Transparent copy along with each Opaque copy, or state in or with each Opaque copy a computer-network location from which the general network-using public has access to download using public-standard network protocols a complete Transparent copy of the Document, free of added material. If you use the latter option, you must take reasonably prudent steps, when you begin distribution of Opaque copies in quantity, to ensure that this Transparent copy will remain thus accessible at the stated location until at least one year after the last time you distribute an Opaque copy (directly or through your agents or retailers) of that edition to the public. It is requested, but not required, that you contact the authors of the Document well before redistributing any large number of copies, to give them a chance to provide you with an updated version of the Document.

4. MODIFICATIONS
You may copy and distribute a Modified Version of the Document under the conditions of sections 2 and 3 above, provided that you release the Modified Version under precisely this License, with the Modified Version filling the role of the Document, thus licensing distribution and modification of the Modified Version to whoever possesses a copy of it. In addition, you must do these things in the Modified Version: A. Use in the Title Page (and on the covers, if any) a title distinct from that of the Document, and from those of previous versions (which should, if there were any, be listed in the History section of the Document). You may use the same title as a previous version if the original publisher of that version gives permission. B. List on the Title Page, as authors, one or more persons or entities responsible for authorship of the modifications in the Modified Version, together with at least five of the principal authors of the Document (all of its principal authors, if it has fewer than five), unless they release you from this requirement. C. State on the Title page the name of the publisher of the Modified Version, as the publisher. D. Preserve all the copyright notices of the Document. E. Add an appropriate copyright notice for your modifications adjacent to the other copyright notices. F. Include, immediately after the copyright notices, a license notice giving the public permission to use the Modified Version under the terms of this License, in the form shown in the Addendum below. G. Preserve in that license notice the full lists of Invariant Sections and required Cover Texts given in the Document's license notice. H. Include an unaltered copy of this License. I. Preserve the section Entitled "History", Preserve its Title, and add to it an item stating at least the title, year, new authors, and publisher of the Modified Version as given on the Title Page. If there is no section Entitled "History" in the Document, create one stating the title, year, authors, and publisher of the Document as given on its Title Page, then add an item describing the Modified Version as stated in the previous sentence. J. Preserve the network location, if any, given in the Document for public access to a Transparent copy of the Document, and likewise the network locations given in the Document for previous versions it was based on. These may be placed in the "History" section. You may omit a network location for a work that was published at least four years before the Document itself, or if the original publisher of the version it refers to gives permission. K. For any section Entitled "Acknowledgements" or "Dedications", Preserve the Title of the section, and preserve in the section all the substance and tone of each of the contributor acknowledgements and/or dedications given therein. L. Preserve all the Invariant Sections of the Document, unaltered in their text and in their titles. Section numbers or the equivalent are not considered part of the section titles. M. Delete any section Entitled "Endorsements". Such a section may not be included in the Modified Version. N. Do not retitle any existing section to be Entitled "Endorsements" or to conflict in title with any Invariant Section. O. Preserve any Warranty Disclaimers. If the Modified Version includes new front-matter sections or appendices that qualify as Secondary Sections and contain no material copied from the Document, you may at your option designate some or all of these sections as invariant. To do this, add their titles to the list of Invariant Sections in the Modified Version's license notice. These titles must be distinct from any other section titles. You may add a section Entitled "Endorsements", provided it contains nothing but endorsements of your Modified Version by various parties--for example, statements of peer review or that the text has been approved by an organization as the authoritative definition of a standard. You may add a passage of up to five words as a Front-Cover Text, and a passage of up to 25 words as a Back-Cover Text, to the end of the list of Cover Texts in the Modified Version. Only one passage of Front-Cover Text and one of Back-Cover Text may be added by (or through arrangements made by) any one entity. If the Document already includes a cover text for the same cover, previously added by you or by arrangement made by the same entity you are acting on behalf of, you may not add another; but you may replace the old one, on explicit permission from the previous publisher that added the old one. The author(s) and publisher(s) of the Document do not by this License give permission to use their names for publicity for or to assert or imply endorsement of any Modified Version.

5. COMBINING DOCUMENTS
You may combine the Document with other documents released under this License, under the terms defined in section 4 above for modified versions, provided that you include in the combination all of the Invariant Sections of all of the original documents, unmodified, and list them all as Invariant Sections of your combined work in its license notice, and that you preserve all their Warranty Disclaimers. The combined work need only contain one copy of this License, and multiple identical Invariant Sections may be replaced with a single copy. If there are multiple Invariant Sections with the same name but different contents, make the title of each such section unique by adding at the end of it, in parentheses, the name of the original author or publisher of that section if known, or else a unique number. Make the same adjustment to the section titles in the list of Invariant Sections in the license notice of the combined work. In the combination, you must combine any sections Entitled "History" in the various original documents, forming one section Entitled "History"; likewise combine any sections Entitled "Acknowledgements", and any sections Entitled "Dedications". You must delete all sections Entitled "Endorsements".

6. COLLECTIONS OF DOCUMENTS
You may make a collection consisting of the Document and other documents released under this License, and replace the individual copies of this License in the various documents with a single copy that is included in the collection, provided that you follow the rules of this License for verbatim copying of each of the documents in all other respects. You may extract a single document from such a collection, and distribute it individually under this License, provided you insert a copy of this License into the extracted document, and follow this License in all other respects regarding verbatim copying of that document.

7. AGGREGATION WITH INDEPENDENT WORKS
A compilation of the Document or its derivatives with other separate and independent documents or works, in or on a volume of a storage or distribution medium, is called an "aggregate" if the copyright resulting from the compilation is not used to limit the legal rights of the compilation's users beyond what the individual works permit. When the Document is included in an aggregate, this License does not apply to the other works in the aggregate which are not themselves derivative works of the Document. If the Cover Text requirement of section 3 is applicable to these copies of the Document, then if the Document is less than one half of the entire aggregate, the Document's Cover Texts may be placed on covers that bracket the Document within the aggregate, or the electronic equivalent of covers if the Document is in electronic form. Otherwise they must appear on printed covers that bracket the whole aggregate.

8. TRANSLATION
Translation is considered a kind of modification, so you may distribute translations of the Document under the terms of section 4. Replacing Invariant Sections with translations requires special permission from their copyright holders, but you may include translations of some or all Invariant Sections in addition to the original versions of these Invariant Sections. You may include a translation of this License, and all the license notices in the Document, and any Warranty Disclaimers, provided that you also include the original English version of this License and the original versions of those notices and disclaimers. In case of a disagreement between the translation and the original version of this License or a notice or disclaimer, the original version will prevail. If a section in the Document is Entitled "Acknowledgements", "Dedications", or "History", the requirement (section 4) to Preserve its Title (section 1) will typically require changing the actual title.

9. TERMINATION
You may not copy, modify, sublicense, or distribute the Document except as expressly provided for under this License. Any other attempt to copy, modify, sublicense or distribute the Document is void, and will automatically terminate your rights under this License. However, parties who have received copies, or rights, from you under this License will not have their licenses terminated so long as such parties remain in full compliance.

10. FUTURE REVISIONS OF THIS LICENSE
The Free Software Foundation may publish new, revised versions of the GNU Free Documentation License from time to time. Such new versions will be similar in spirit to the present version, but may differ in detail to address new problems or concerns. See http://www.gnu.org/copyleft/. Each version of the License is given a distinguishing version number. If the Document specifies that a particular numbered version of this License "or any later version" applies to it, you have the option of following the terms and conditions either of that specified version or of any later version that has been published (not as a draft) by the Free Software Foundation. If the Document does not specify a version number of this License, you may choose any version ever published (not as a draft) by the Free Software Foundation. ADDENDUM: How to use this License for your documents To use this License in a document you have written, include a copy of the License in the document and put the following copyright and license notices just after the title page: Copyright (c) YEAR YOUR NAME. Permission is granted to copy, distribute and/or modify this document under the terms of the GNU Free Documentation License, Version 1.2 or any later version published by the Free Software Foundation; with no Invariant Sections, no Front-Cover Texts, and no Back-Cover Texts. A copy of the license is included in the section entitled "GNU Free Documentation License". If you have Invariant Sections, Front-Cover Texts and Back-Cover Texts, replace the "with...Texts." line with this: with the Invariant Sections being LIST THEIR TITLES, with the Front-Cover Texts being LIST, and with the Back-Cover Texts being LIST. If you have Invariant Sections without Cover Texts, or some other combination of the three, merge those two alternatives to suit the situation. If your document contains nontrivial examples of program code, we recommend releasing these examples in parallel under your choice of free software license, such as the GNU General Public License, to permit their use in free software.

Printed by Books on Demand GmbH, Norderstedt / Germany